FIRST LADIES
OF THE
WHITE HOUSE

BY NANCY J. SKARMEAS

ISBN 0-8249-4200-0

Copyright © 2000 by Ideals Publications, a division of Guideposts

All rights reserved. No part of this publication may be reproduced or transmitted in any form or by any means, electronic or mechanical, including photocopy, recording, or any information storage or retrieval system, without permission in writing from the publisher.

Printed and bound in the U.S.A. by RR Donnelly & Sons.

Published by Ideals Publications
a division of Guideposts
535 Metroplex Drive, Suite 250
Nashville, TN 37211

Library of Congress Cataloging-in-Publication Data
Skarmeas, Nancy J.
    First ladies of the White House / by Nancy Skarmeas.
    p. cm.
    Includes index.
    ISBN 0-8249-4200-0 (alk. paper)
    1. Presidents' spouses—United States—Biography. 2. Presidents' spouses—United States—Pictorial works. I. Title.

E176.2.S58 2000
973'.09'9—dc21
[B]   00-047147

1 0 8 6 4 2 1 3 5 7 9

Publisher, Patricia A. Pingry
Designer, Travis Rader
Copy Editor, Elizabeth Kea
Editorial Assistant, Amy Johnson

FIRST LADIES
OF THE
WHITE HOUSE

By Nancy J. Skarmeas

"I, and yet, not I—
this was the wife of the
President of the United States
and she took precedence
over me...."

GRACE GOODHUE COOLIDGE

IDEALS PUBLICATIONS, A DIVISION OF GUIDEPOSTS

NASHVILLE, TENNESSEE

WWW.IDEALSPUBLICATIONS.COM

Martha Dandridge Custis Washington
1731–1802
George Washington Administration 1789–1797

Martha Washington looked forward to a quiet, private retirement after the Revolutionary War ended and her husband, General George Washington, resigned his commission as commander in chief of the colonial army. We will "grow old together in solitude and tranquility," she wrote as they settled in at their beautiful Mount Vernon estate in Virginia. But in just four short years, Mrs. Washington's quiet world was turned upside down. In 1789, George Washington was elected the first president of the United States of America; and Martha Washington, almost sixty years old, found herself beginning a new life as America's leading lady.

Martha Dandridge was born on June 2, 1731, in New Kent County, Virginia. She lived a happy and active childhood on her father's profitable plantation. As was the custom for girls of her day, Martha received no formal education in academic subjects but was schooled soundly in the domestic arts. When she was still a teenager, Martha married Daniel Parke Custis, a wealthy tobacco heir twenty years her senior. They had four children, two of whom survived infancy, before Custis died eight years later leaving Martha a young and very wealthy widow. At twenty-five, Martha Custis took responsibility for her deceased husband's 17,000-acre estate, however, she was not to be alone for long. On January 6, 1759, Martha married an ambitious young officer named George Washington.

When George became commander in chief of the colonial army during the Revolutionary War, his wife joined him in the battle for American independence. She helped enlist nurses and organize collections of warm clothing for the soldiers. Mrs. Washington was a frequent visitor to her husband in camp, where she helped with his correspondence, discussed plans for battle, and did much by her mere presence to raise the spirits of the troops.

Although Martha Washington became a beloved and recognized public figure during the Revolutionary War, she remained a very private person; and her husband's election to the presidency filled her with trepidation. Popularity was familiar to her, but as the wife of the president she was to have a public role—one which was entirely undefined. An elegant, graceful woman with the bearing of her aristocratic Virginia roots, Martha Washington was criticized as too "royal" by some Americans wary of all things British. At the same time, she was decried as too common by those who feared that her habits of recycling old gowns and of retiring early during receptions might confirm the suspicions of the world that America was an uncivilized wilderness. But to all who visited the president's house—in New York City or later in Philadelphia—Lady Washington was the model of grace and propriety; eventually, these qualities won her the affection and respect of all America.

In 1797, it was with pleasure that Martha retired with George once more to Mount Vernon. In her later years she became the grande dame of American politics—a visit to Martha at Mount Vernon was considered a prerequisite for all those with political ambitions. She died in May of 1802. The Washingtons are buried at Mount Vernon.

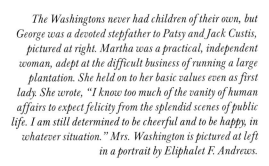

The Washingtons never had children of their own, but George was a devoted stepfather to Patsy and Jack Custis, pictured at right. Martha was a practical, independent woman, adept at the difficult business of running a large plantation. She held on to her basic values even as first lady. She wrote, "I know too much of the vanity of human affairs to expect felicity from the splendid scenes of public life. I am still determined to be cheerful and to be happy, in whatever situation." Mrs. Washington is pictured at left in a portrait by Eliphalet F. Andrews.

ABIGAIL SMITH ADAMS

1744–1818

JOHN ADAMS ADMINISTRATION 1797–1801

Our second first lady was as reluctant to take on the role as our first, but for different reasons. Martha Washington regretted the loss of her privacy; Abigail Adams regretted the loss of her freedom. Mrs. Adams was a woman of strong opinions, used to speaking her mind freely with her husband and his colleagues on social and political issues. She feared that the role pioneered by Martha Washington required patience, tolerance, and discretion beyond her own. Mrs. Washington, ever the gracious hostess and loyal wife, had gladly left the political spotlight to her husband; Mrs. Adams wondered whether she could do the same.

Born in Weymouth, Massachusetts, in November of 1744 to two of New England's most established families, Abigail Smith, like most eighteenth-century colonial women, received no formal education. Through a determined course of independent reading—she studied philosophy, Latin, literature, and history—she made herself one of the best-educated women in the colonies. At eighteen, Abigail began a courtship with John Adams, an aspiring lawyer. The two were well-matched—both bright, outspoken, and stubborn. They married in 1764 and settled in Braintree, Massachusetts, where John pursued his interests in law and colonial politics and Abigail ran their farm and raised their children, six of whom were born in the first seven years of marriage.

In the years to come, as John Adams rose to prominence as a leader of the Revolution and the emerging nation, Abigail remained in Braintree with the children, except during John Adams's term as minister to England, when she relocated with him to London. To ease the loneliness of their separation, Abigail began a correspondence with her husband that often reached three letters a day. Through their letters, Abigail and John Adams kept informed of each other's daily lives, and Abigail shared her opinions on her husband's work and the issues of the day.

Abigail Adams was not entirely happy as first lady. As she feared, it was a difficult role for a woman of her outspoken temperament, and she never found the satisfaction in the role of hostess that Martha Washington had enjoyed. It was no secret that John Adams consulted his wife on important decisions, and many believed Abigail's role went far beyond mere consultation. Mrs. Adams was called "Mrs. President" and "Her Majesty" by some who thought her too outspoken for a woman; she ignored their remarks and continued to advise her husband and attend meetings of the House of Representatives. Abigail Adams loved the business of politics and government, but she could not escape the truth that in American society her involvement in both was dependent upon her husband.

When John Adams's bid for reelection proved unsuccessful, he and Abigail retired to Massachusetts. Abigail died in 1818, seven years before her own son, John Quincy Adams, became the sixth president of the United States.

Abigail Adams was one of America's first voices for women's rights. Her letters to her husband reveal strong beliefs about the issue of equality—beliefs out of sync with the prevailing attitudes in colonial America. In perhaps her most often quoted letter, Abigail urged John, who was serving in the Continental Congress, to "remember the Ladies, and be more generous and favorable than your ancestors."

MARTHA WAYLES SKELTON JEFFERSON
1748–1782
THOMAS JEFFERSON ADMINISTRATION 1801–1809

Martha Wayles Skelton Jefferson, born in Williamsburg, Virginia, in 1748, did not live to see her husband, Thomas Jefferson, elected third president of the United States of America. After seven difficult pregnancies in ten years of marriage, Mrs. Jefferson died in 1782 at the age of thirty-four. Legend has it that Mrs. Jefferson's last wish was that her husband not marry again, as would have been the custom for a widower of his time. Whether or not this is true, Thomas Jefferson was deeply saddened by the loss of his wife and lived the remainder of his days a single man.

As president, Jefferson relied upon his only two surviving children—daughters Martha and Mary—and the wife of a cabinet member to fulfill the role of official White House hostess. It was Martha, or "Patsy," who took on the principle duties of hostess during her father's two terms. Married to her second cousin, Thomas Mann Randolph, Patsy had spent much of her childhood in Europe with her father while he served as minister in Paris and was a well-educated and sophisticated woman by the time her father became the president. Although she eventually had children of her own and a household to manage in Virginia, Patsy managed to spend as much time as possible at the White House with her father and would often live with him during the busy social season. Her sister "Polly" often stood in as hostess as well, and both young women received guidance and support from Dolley Madison, the wife of Jefferson's secretary of state. Dolley often took on the role of White House hostess during the Jefferson administration when his daughters were unavailable. Patsy Jefferson Randolph remained her father's devoted companion after his retirement until his death. In his will, Jefferson entrusted his beloved Monticello estate to her care.

This silhouette is the only surviving likeness of Martha Wayles Skelton Jefferson, the wife of third president Thomas Jefferson. Jefferson was Martha Wayles's second husband. At eighteen she had married Bathurst Skelton, who died only two years later, shortly after the tragic death of their infant son. After Martha's death, Jefferson was so stricken by grief that he refused to leave his room for three weeks. He later destroyed all of his wife's letters and any other reminders of her.

Named for her mother, Martha "Patsy" Jefferson bore a striking resemblance to her father, third president Thomas Jefferson, to whom she was devoted throughout her lifetime. Patsy, pictured here in an eighteenth-century engraving, was educated at a convent school in Paris until her father, fearing that she would convert to Catholicism, removed her from the tutelage of the French nuns. Patsy Randolph's two surviving sons continued their grandfather's tradition of public service. Thomas Jefferson Randolph served in the Virginia state legislature. His brother George Wythe Randolph was secretary of war for the Confederacy during the Civil War.

DOLLEY PAYNE MADISON
1768–1849
JAMES MADISON ADMINISTRATION 1809–1817

Martha Washington and Abigail Adams were reluctant first ladies; they always believed themselves to be unsuited to the public role. Patsy Jefferson Randolph loyally stood by her widower father during his two terms out of a sense of love and loyalty. But Dolley Madison, wife of the fourth president James Madison, embraced her role at the White House. Mrs. Madison brought a spirit and strength to Washington that are admired to this day. Unlike her predecessors, Dolley Madison seemed born to be the first lady.

Born in 1768 to John and Mary Payne, Dolley, one of nine children, was raised a Quaker, first on a plantation in Virginia and later, after John Payne freed his slaves and found his plantation no longer profitable, in Philadelphia. Dolley married John Todd in 1790, but within three years found herself a widow with a young son. Not long after, she met James Madison, seventeen years her senior; they were married in 1794.

As first lady, Dolley Madison was a composite of her two earliest predecessors. Like Martha Washington, she enjoyed her duties as homemaker and hostess; like Abigail Adams, she had strong political opinions and was a trusted advisor to her husband. But unlike either, Dolley Madison did not struggle with the conflict between her public and private roles; she blended the two with confidence. Mrs. Madison was a vivacious, warmhearted woman with a genuine love of people and a flair for entertaining. When James Madison began his presidency, his wife had already had eight years of training for her role while serving as occasional hostess for Thomas Jefferson. As first lady in her own right, she quickly became known for her lively receptions, including the first ever inaugural ball and regular Wednesday night gatherings that drew the most influential people in Washington. Women across America emulated Dolley's gowns, her jewelry, her hats, even her choice of pets—Mrs. Madison's pet macaw began a nationwide craze for parrots. In contrast to her serious, soft-spoken husband—whose popularity suffered during the difficult days of the War of 1812—Dolley was embraced by nearly all of Washington society and the American public. Her spirit and optimism gave a lift to the capital city during the dark days of the War of 1812.

Mrs. Madison's most memorable moment as first lady came during the war as the British marched on Washington in August of 1814. Dolley, alone at the White House, stood her ground, determined to await the safe return of her husband. Despite the boasting of the British troops that they would take Mrs. Madison as their hostage, she resisted all warnings to flee the city. When she finally did leave, she took with her drafts of the Constitution and the Declaration of Independence, the national seal, and a Gilbert Stuart painting of George Washington. Only hours later, the house was burned to the ground by British troops, and Dolley, already a national favorite, was a national heroine.

When James Madison left office, Dolley retired with him to Montpelier, their Virginia estate; but after his death in 1836, she returned to the city she loved, Washington, D.C. There she once again became the nation's most popular hostess and a valued source of advice and support to subsequent first ladies. When she died in 1849, Dolley Madison was remembered with an elaborate funeral attended by America's greatest living leaders, including President Zachary Taylor, who in his eulogy for Mrs. Madison uttered the title that all future presidents' wives would officially inherit: "she will never be forgotten, because she was truly our First Lady for a half-century."

Before President Zachary Taylor used the term "First Lady" in reference to Dolley Madison, the president's wife had no official title. Martha Washington had been respectfully called "Lady Washington." Abigail Adams also went by the title "Lady," although many thought "Mrs. President" more fitting due to her political involvement. Elizabeth Monroe preferred simply "Mrs. Monroe," but in the press and around Washington she was called "Queen Elizabeth" because of her refined tastes and manners. In her own lifetime, Dolley Madison was addressed as the "Lady Presidentress"; Julia Tyler took this one step further and became the "Lovely Lady Presidentress" in all written references. But within a decade of Zachary Taylor's 1849 eulogy, "First Lady" had become the standard; today it remains the official title of the president's spouse.

Elizabeth Monroe may have had refined tastes and the manners of a wealthy, New York upbringing, but much of the criticism that she endured was due to behaviors likely caused by her poor health. Her husband wrote that she suffered "convulsions that kept her unconscious"; and at one point she is reported to have fallen into a burning fireplace, causing herself serious injury. Because the Monroes were so secretive about the first lady's illness, however, and because medicine of the day offered little hope for sufferers of epilepsy, Elizabeth Monroe suffered silently, and her public image remained that of a distant and inaccessible woman.

ELIZABETH KORTRIGHT MONROE

1768–1830

JAMES MONROE ADMINISTRATION 1817–1825

After sixteen years at the center of Washington society—eight as occasional fill-in hostess during the administration of Thomas Jefferson and eight during her own husband's presidency—Dolley Madison left some very large shoes to fill for the next woman to occupy the White House, Elizabeth Kortright Monroe. The wife of fifth president James Monroe, Elizabeth did not fill those shoes. In fact, she did not even try.

The change in Washington from the Madison years could be felt the very day of James Monroe's inauguration, when his wife Elizabeth was nowhere to be seen at the official reception at their private home following the ceremony. The White House was still undergoing renovations made necessary by the fire of August 1814; Washingtonians wondered if perhaps Mrs. Monroe was waiting to make her debut at the official residence. But the new first lady did not leave the people of Washington guessing for long. Through her daughter, Eliza Hay, Elizabeth Monroe sent the word out that she would not maintain Mrs. Madison's tradition of making or receiving social calls in Washington. Mrs. Hay greeted visitors one morning a week at the White House, but the wife of the president remained aloof. The unveiling of the newly decorated White House on New Year's Day 1818 did little to improve Mrs. Monroe's reputation. The decor was extravagant and very French—elegant, certainly, but excessive and too European for average American tastes. Elizabeth Monroe, off on the wrong foot almost immediately, would never win the affections of the American public.

Tall, graceful, and beautiful, Elizabeth Kortright was born and raised in New York City, the daughter of a wealthy British officer and merchant. She met James Monroe when he was a member of the Continental Congress. They married in February of 1786 and together had two daughters. Elizabeth was a strong-willed, domineering woman who exercised powerful control over her husband. During their years in Paris while James served as minister, Elizabeth achieved great popularity with the French people for her open admiration and emulation of their culture and customs. So influential was Mrs. Monroe in Paris that she was able to secure the release of Madame de Lafayette from a French prison following the French Revolution. As first lady, however, Mrs. Monroe found that the European sophistication that had won her praise in France garnered only scorn in Washington. Her influence was limited to her husband, who struggled to balance the demands of his wife with those of his office.

Elizabeth Monroe was a complex character, perhaps misunderstood by her contemporaries and history. She often cited an unidentified illness as the reason for her reclusiveness, and some historians have speculated that she suffered from the little understood disease of epilepsy, which would explain her infrequent public appearances and her husband's protectiveness. Whatever the reason, Elizabeth Monroe was fiercely independent and seemingly unconcerned with conforming to public expectations. Dubbed "Queen Elizabeth" by those who thought her haughty attitude unfitting for her position, Mrs. Monroe did win some increased popularity during her husband's second term, but she never adapted her behavior in pursuit of popularity. Her predecessors had either seen the public obligations of their role as a duty or a pleasure; Elizabeth Monroe simply chose to ignore these obligations. She died in 1830 at the Monroes' Oak Hill estate in Virginia.

LOUISA JOHNSON ADAMS
1775–1852
JOHN QUINCY ADAMS ADMINISTRATION 1825–1829

Louisa Adams campaigned long and hard for her husband prior to the presidential election of 1824. She met with the wives of congressmen, hosted sixty-eight separate dinners for members of the House and the Senate, and, in a shrewd public relations move, even put together a ball in honor of her husband's opponent, General Andrew Jackson. When John Quincy Adams won the presidency, however, Louisa found that what she had won were four of the most trying years of her life. For the intelligent and talented Louisa Adams, life as first lady turned out to be confining and difficult.

Setting up residence at the White House should have been a welcome move for Louisa Adams. Born in London in 1775 to a British mother and an American father, Louisa Johnson met John Quincy Adams when both were still children. They married in 1797 and for the next twenty-eight years moved continually across Europe, the United States, and even to St. Petersburg, Russia, to follow John Quincy Adams's career as a diplomat. Louisa, mother of three sons, only one of whom outlived her, had suffered ill health and several miscarriages; a settled life seemed just what she needed. But for this British-born woman, the White House was more of a prison than a refuge.

John Quincy Adams, elected by the narrowest of margins, was consumed by the need to win and maintain political support. He was a tireless worker, with little time for his wife or children. In fact, he once remarked that a woman with intellectual abilities suffered a true handicap, for she was destined to be disappointed with her lot in life. For Louisa, his theory proved correct. She suffered periods of depression in the White House and lived her four years there mostly in seclusion. She did enjoy occasional entertaining and playing the piano, but for the most part her Washington years were lonely and disappointing. To make matters worse, she continually struggled under the disapproval of her mother-in-law, Abigail Adams, who always believed her son should have married an American-born woman. Louisa also experienced the tragedy of the suicide of one of her sons.

The Adams presidency was unsuccessful and, thankfully for Louisa, limited to one term. For both the Adamses, the years after their White House days were to prove among the most fruitful of their lives. After years of distance in their marriage, John and Louisa Adams finally found a common cause in the fight for the abolition of slavery. While her husband worked toward the end of slavery as a member of the House of Representatives, Louisa served as his zealous assistant. Louisa Adams died in 1852 and is buried alongside her husband in Quincy, Massachusetts.

Louisa Johnson met John Quincy Adams for the first time when she was four years old. The Johnson family's home was in London, but they had taken refuge in Nantes, France, when the American Revolution made it unwise for her father, an American businessman, to remain in England. Twelve-year-old John Quincy Adams was in Nantes as part of a European tour with his father. Louisa and John met again years later in London, where Louisa's father served as American consul, and it was there that their courtship and marriage took place. Although Abigail Adams never truly accepted her son's choice of a foreign-born wife, John Adams is said to have been quite close to his daughter-in-law.

"There is something in this great unsocial house," wrote Louisa Adams of the White House, "which depresses my spirits beyond expression and makes it impossible for me to feel at home or to fancy that I have a home anywhere." Her husband was little comfort: "Family is and must ever be secondary consideration to a zealous patriot," she wrote of John Quincy Adams's obsession with his work. Louisa turned to solitude, music, and writing to relieve the depression that darkened her days in the White House, but it was not until the 1840s that she was to find a source of inspiration and satisfaction in her fight for the abolition of slavery.

RACHEL DONELSON JACKSON
1767–1828
ANDREW JACKSON ADMINISTRATION 1829–1837

Rachel Jackson died just three weeks before her husband's inauguration as seventh president of the United States, but her presence was felt throughout Andrew Jackson's administration. An independent, strong-minded man, President Jackson was fiercely loyal to the memory of his late wife and sorely unforgiving of those who had failed to give her the respect she deserved.

Rachel Donelson was born in 1767 in Halifax County, Virginia, but she spent much of her youth on the rugged Tennessee and Kentucky frontier. She met Andrew Jackson at her mother's home in Nashville, Tennessee. The two fell in love, but because Rachel was legally married to Lewis Robards—an abusive man who in a fit of jealousy had sent her back to her mother from the couple's home in Kentucky—they did not act upon their feelings. When Robards declared that he would divorce Rachel, she and Jackson married. They believed that the divorce was official and Rachel was free. Later they learned that Robards had not acted on his threat of divorce until two years after their marriage, which made Rachel, by law, guilty of adultery. Although she and Jackson immediately remarried to rectify the legalities of their situation, the misunderstanding was to haunt them all of their days.

Rachel Jackson was a generous, unpretentious woman little interested in the social life of Washington. She urged her husband to give up his ambitions for public office and remain at the Hermitage, their home in Nashville, but Jackson could not resist the allure of the presidency. During his unsuccessful first campaign against John Quincy Adams, Rachel's character became an issue, and whispers of a "scandalous" past spread throughout Washington. During the second campaign four years later, the whispers became bold public statements; the secret of Rachel's past was revealed, and her character became the focus of the campaign. Andrew Jackson boldly defended his wife and emerged victorious despite the scandal; but the strain of public criticism may have been too much for his wife. Rachel Jackson suffered a fatal heart attack in December of 1828, only weeks before her husband was to begin his presidency.

Andrew Jackson always blamed the brutal personal attacks of the campaign for his wife's death. "I

Although Rachel Jackson was less than enthusiastic about her husband's presidential ambitions, her reluctance stemmed from disinterest and not social incompetence. As a child she had met Presidents Washington and Jefferson and traveled extensively in the East with her father, a member of the Virginia House of Burgesses. As an adult, however, she valued family and home above all else. In a letter to her husband, she wrote, "do not let the love of country, fame, and honor make your forget [your family] . . . You will say this is not the language of a patriot, but it is the language of a faithful wife."

can and do forgive all my enemies," he remarked upon assuming office, "but those vile wretches who have slandered her must look to God for mercy." Social duties at the White House were taken on by Emily Donelson, the wife of Andrew's nephew, and Sarah Jackson, the wife of Andrew and Rachel's adopted son, Andrew Jackson, Jr. Another woman, Peggy Eaton, the wife of Secretary of War John Eaton, also filled a social role at Jackson's White House. Mrs. Eaton, who was rumored to have been pregnant before her marriage to John Eaton, became the center of much controversy during the Jackson years. She suffered personal attacks much like those that had assailed Mrs. Jackson and was ostracized from Washington society. Andrew Jackson passionately defended Mrs. Eaton, and what became known as "the Peggy Eaton affair" was at the heart of his conflict with his own cabinet, a conflict so severe as to cause him to abandon regular cabinet meetings and seek counsel instead from a group of personal advisors. At the heart of his defense of Mrs. Eaton must have been his bitterness over the treatment his wife had received. In personal affairs as in those political, Andrew Jackson was loyal and strong-willed; the memory of Rachel Jackson was one of the guiding lights of his presidency.

HANNAH HOES VAN BUREN
1783–1819
MARTIN VAN BUREN ADMINISTRATION 1837–1841

Hannah Hoes Van Buren, the childhood sweetheart and wife of eighth president Martin Van Buren, died nearly twenty years before her husband was elected to the presidency. Mrs. Van Buren, like her husband the child of Dutch parents and a native of Kinderhook, New York, did, however, give her husband four sons before she succumbed to tuberculosis after twelve years of marriage. It was one of those sons, Abraham, who, with the help of former first lady Dolley Madison, provided President Van Buren with a White House hostess, a young woman from South Carolina who made a significant impression during her short reign as lady of the White House.

After the death of her husband James in 1836, Dolley Madison returned to Washington to live in a house just across from the White House. She was a close friend of the new president, Martin Van Buren, and occasionally filled her old familiar role of hostess for his White House receptions. Seeing the need for a more permanent "woman's touch" in the president's home, where Van Buren lived with his four bachelor sons, Mrs. Madison arranged for her young cousin Angelica Singleton to make the trip up from South Carolina to meet the Van Burens. A match was soon made between Abraham Van Buren and Mrs. Madison's cousin, and with their marriage Angelica assumed the official role of White House hostess.

Angelica, raised in luxury on her family's large southern plantation, embraced her new role. Whereas Martin Van Buren, though elegant and formal, had tried to live frugally in the White House, Angelica had different ideas. After a honeymoon trip to Europe, she came back to Washington with her head full of royal palaces and ceremonies. Like her cousin Dolley Madison, Angelica loved to entertain; unlike Dolley, however, her tastes ran toward the extravagant and her manners toward the pretentious. Angelica, who loved to dress in royal purple, ultimately proved a part of President Van Buren's downfall. In his battle for reelection against William Henry Harrison, who portrayed himself as the "man-of-the-people," Van Buren appeared overly refined; and the extravagant White House practices of his daughter-in-law became the focus of much negative attention. Van Buren lost the election to Harrison, and Angelica's short time at the White House ended. After leaving the capital, Angelica and Abraham settled in New York City, where she died in 1878.

Because Hannah Hoes Van Buren, right, died before her husband entered the White House, her daughter-in-law, Angelica, fulfilled her role. At her first public appearance as official White House hostess on January 1, 1839, Angelica Van Buren won rave reviews. A newspaper account of the New Year's Day reception called the new lady of the house a woman "of rare accomplishments . . . universally admired." Angelica's honeymoon with the public did not last too long after her own European honeymoon with her new husband later that spring, however. The first White House hostess to tour Europe, Angelica was received like a queen by foreign heads of state and returned believing herself to be one. Before long, Angelica, like her father-in-law, found herself out of favor and out of the White House.

ANNA TUTHILL SYMMES HARRISON
1775–1864
WILLIAM HENRY HARRISON ADMINISTRATION 1841

Legend has it that during the Revolutionary War, colonist John Cleves Symmes dressed as a British redcoat and rode across enemy lines to carry his infant daughter from their home in New Jersey to the safety of her grandparents' home on Long Island. It was there that his daughter, Anna Tuthill Symmes, born in 1775, grew up and–through the devoted tutoring of her grandmother–received a solid education. When her father moved west to Ohio to settle on a five-hundred-thousand-acre estate near Cincinnati some years later, Anna, by then a teenager, followed. She met her future husband, William Henry Harrison, a career army officer, in Lexington, Kentucky, in 1795. Despite her father's objections–Mr. Symmes believed that Harrison was more devoted to his military career than to his daughter and that the rugged life of an army wife was not in her best interests–Anna secretly married Harrison on November 25, 1795, in North Bend, Ohio.

John Symmes had been right about one thing: Anna's life with William Henry Harrison was never to be easy. While William pursued his career as an army officer and later as a public official in the Northwest Territory, Anna moved with him from one post to the next. She focused her energies on home and family–managing the chores of farming and raising their ten children. Because schools in the frontier territory were few and far between, Anna also took on the responsibility of educating her own children and often those of their neighbors. She was a deeply religious woman who relied heavily upon her faith for strength and courage during the many difficult, lonely years of her marriage.

When William Henry Harrison was elected to the presidency in 1840, he was nearly seventy years old. Anna had objected to his campaign, for she wished that he would come home instead and live his last years in quiet retirement. She did not travel to Washington for his inauguration; she planned instead to make her way east in May, when the weather improved. Mrs. Harrison sent her daughter-in-law Jane to Washington to serve as her husband's temporary hostess. Anna Harrison never made the trip to the capital; after only one month in office, President Harrison died and Vice-President John Tyler assumed the presidency.

Anna Harrison lived two decades after her husband's death and survived all but one of her ten children. As she had all her life, she kept up a keen interest in politics and, during her last years, urged her grandson Benjamin Harrison to fight for the Union in the Civil War. She did not, however, live to see him win the presidency. Anna Harrison died in 1864 and is buried next to her husband at the site of their North Bend, Ohio, home.

Like so many of our earliest first ladies, Anna Harrison did not want her husband to become the president. "I wish," she said of his candidacy, "that my husband's friends had left him where he was, happy and contented in retirement." But Mrs. Harrison, for all her objections to her husband's continued political involvement, was an intelligent and informed woman who maintained an active interest in politics. Isolated much of her life on the frontier with her children, she nonetheless read magazines and newspapers voraciously and looked forward to the visits from her husband's colleagues, which gave her the opportunity to engage her love of political conversation.

19

LETITIA CHRISTIAN TYLER
1790–1842
JOHN TYLER ADMINISTRATION 1841–1845

During their courtship, John Tyler wrote to Letitia Christian, "Whether I float or sink in the stream of fortune, you may be assured of this, that I shall never cease to love you." The object of Tyler's devotion was a quiet, pious, young woman, born at Cedar Grove Plantation in Virginia in November of 1790. The couple married in 1813, beginning a union of twenty-nine years, during which they were blessed with eight children, seven of whom survived to maturity.

By the time John Tyler assumed the presidency in 1841 upon the death of William Henry Harrison, Letitia, who had suffered a paralytic stroke, was confined to her bed. During her White House days, she remained, for the most part, in the family quarters of the White House, where she read, knitted, and advised her children and her husband. Nonetheless hers was a palpable and positive influence over life in the White House. Letitia had been a skilled businesswoman in her earlier days and had managed the family plantation and finances. Whereas her stroke had affected her physically, it had left her mentally as bright and sharp as ever. As first lady, she remained her husband's closest confidante and kept her eye on all family matters. Although there were rumors that she made an occasional secret trip to the theater, Letitia Christian made only one official public appearance during her time in the White House—for her daughter Elizabeth's wedding in January of 1842. The first lady died that September following a second stroke and is buried at Cedar Grove.

Letitia Tyler, pictured above, handed over her duties as White House hostess to her daughter-in-law, Priscilla Cooper Tyler, who, as a former actress, was well-suited to the role. But the elder Mrs. Tyler always remained in control of family life in the White House. John Tyler was especially devoted to his wife, and he frequently remarked that her guidance and financial management were the cornerstones of his political success. "All her actions," he observed, "are founded on prudence."

It was an explosion aboard the navy ship Princeton that gave Julia Gardiner the final push toward accepting the marriage proposal of President John Tyler in 1844. On February 28 of that year, Julia and her family had joined the president and some four hundred other guests for a cruise on the Potomac River. The highlight of the day was to be the firing of the "Peacemaker," the world's largest cannon. The first firings went off without a hitch, but in late afternoon, the cannon backfired. Julia's father, Senator Gardiner from New York, was killed in the explosion. When Julia fainted, it was President Tyler himself who carried her to safety. From that day on, their courtship moved quickly; in June they were married. The second Mrs. Tyler is pictured at right.

JULIA GARDINER TYLER
1820–1889
JOHN TYLER ADMINISTRATION 1841–1845

Young, vivacious, and extroverted Julia Gardiner first met President John Tyler in 1842. The daughter of prominent New York State Senator David Gardiner and a member of a family with great wealth and connections, Julia had shocked her family and friends by posing for a department store advertisement at age nineteen. She was to give them a much greater shock in 1844 when she agreed to marry President John Tyler, thirty years her senior, less than two years after the death of his first wife. Julia had at first refused the president's proposal. After a terrible explosion killed her father, Julia grew close to John Tyler; and she eventually accepted his proposal of marriage. They were wed in a private ceremony in New York on June 26, 1844, which made John Tyler the first sitting United States president to be married.

Julia Tyler brought great changes to the White House in the short eight months she was to preside as first lady. Younger than some of John Tyler's own daughters, she was controversial both inside the family and out, but she left little doubt in anyone's mind that the role of president's wife was one she was happy to fill. She loved the spotlight and made every attempt to turn the White House into her own royal court. She rode about in a carriage pulled by six white Arabian horses and was attended at all times by twelve personal maids. Known as the "Lovely Lady Presidentress," Julia initiated the practice of playing "Hail to the Chief" at the president's entrance and hosted many formal balls, one with a guest list of over three thousand. She also exerted great political influence on President Tyler, and it was publicly acknowledged that he valued her opinion greatly on all matters, personal and professional.

After John Tyler left office, he and Julia went on to have seven children of their own. During the Civil War, Julia, by 1862 a widow, once again became the center of controversy as she openly supported the Confederacy while living with her family in New York. Julia Tyler died in 1889. She is buried beside the president at Hollywood Cemetery in Richmond, Virginia.

Sarah Polk was driven by her powerful belief that all men and women had roles in the world that had been predestined for them by God. Filling the roles of president and first lady was to her not a reflection of her and her husband's individual achievement but rather a manifestation of God's choice for them. "The greater the prosperity the deeper the sense of gratitude to the Almighty," she once wrote. With a precarious balance of ego and humility, Sarah Polk had absolute confidence and wielded her power and influence liberally, yet all the while insisted: "I recognize nothing in myself; I am only an atom in the hands of God."

SARAH CHILDRESS POLK
1803–1891
JAMES POLK ADMINISTRATION 1845–1849

Unlike so many first ladies before her, Sarah Childress Polk wanted nothing more than for her husband to become president of the United States. Unlike so many of her predecessors, however, Sarah Polk did not envision a White House life full only of endless social occasions and obligations; rather, the bright, outspoken, opinionated, and ambitious Mrs. Polk looked forward to sharing in the work of running the nation. Sarah and James Polk brought to Washington something the American people were not used to seeing: a marriage that was a true partnership of equals.

Born in 1803 in Murfreesboro, Tennessee, Sarah Childress grew up a strict and devout Presbyterian. She was well-educated for a woman of her day, and she met young James Polk while both were students of the same tutor. Full of ambition, but equally aware of the limited prospects for American women in public life in the early nineteenth century, Sarah Childress channeled her energy and ambition into the political career of James Polk. The two were married in 1824; from that day forward they devoted their combined energies almost entirely to the advancement of James's political career.

When the Polks moved into the White House in 1845, Sarah immediately made her presence felt. Her strict religious beliefs eventually led her to ban all dancing, card playing, and drinking in the president's home. "To dance in these rooms would be undignified," she remarked. During her husband's inaugural ball, when the new first lady entered the room, the music and dancing ceased in her honor. Sarah Polk also let it be known that she was not to concern herself with the purely social functions that had either intimidated or delighted her predecessors. Her focus was to be on her husband and the work before him. Sarah Polk was the initial first lady to play a truly active and acknowledged role in her husband's administration. She served as his personal assistant and daily read and highlighted his newspapers, thus letting the president know where his attention should be focused. Sarah Polk loved to talk politics, and she did so with skill and intelligence. Outspoken and judgmental, but always aware of the political consequences of her words and actions, she soon became an influential figure in Washington. So devoted were the Polks to the work of the presidency that they did not take a single vacation during their White House years. Socializing did not cease during the Polk administration, for Sarah, despite her strict ways, loved expensive and elegant gowns; but work always came first.

James Polk is remembered best for his support of Manifest Destiny—the belief that America was chosen by God to rule the continent from the Atlantic to the Pacific. Sarah Polk also believed in destiny; she often told friends that she believed that she and James were predestined by God to lead America. Such absolute confidence in her own mission earned Sarah Polk much respect in Washington, but it also elicited the criticism of many who believed she had strayed far beyond the accepted realm of a woman.

After four years of almost relentless work in the White House, James Polk died just months into his retirement. Sarah lived another forty-two years at the couple's home in Nashville. The Polks had no children; their legacy instead was their working partnership in the White House.

MARGARET MACKALL SMITH TAYLOR
1788–1852
ZACHARY TAYLOR ADMINISTRATION 1849–1850

Peggy Taylor did not sit for a portrait or a photograph during her brief term as first lady—evidence of her total commitment to maintaining her privacy while in the White House. She was not, however, uninvolved in her husband's administration. She regularly received guests, both personal and political, in the family quarters of the White House and worked her own quiet brand of influence on Washington. In public, however, it was her daughter, Betty Bliss, pictured at left, who filled the role of official White House hostess.

Much like Martha Washington and Anna Harrison before her, Margaret Taylor was looking forward to a peaceful retirement with her husband when she found herself instead headed for Washington, D.C. and the White House. Her husband, Zachary Taylor—"Old Rough and Ready"—was a national hero after the Mexican War; he was nominated and elected to the presidency in 1848 with little effort of his own and very much against the private wishes of his wife. When news of her husband's nomination to the presidency reached Mrs. Taylor, she is said to have remarked that it was a "plot to deprive me of his society and shorten his life by unnecessary cares and responsibility."

Margaret Mackall Smith was born in 1788 and raised in a wealthy, refined atmosphere in Calvert County, Maryland. She met Zachary Taylor in 1809 while she was visiting her sister in Kentucky. After her

marriage to Taylor in June of 1810, Margaret, who was often called Peggy, left the comforts of her childhood behind to live the rugged life of the frontier. She moved from fort to fort following her husband's military career. Zachary Taylor once remarked that his wife was "as much a soldier as I," a tribute to her courage and fortitude during long, hard years of raising children amid constant moves, Indian raids, isolation, and separation. The Taylors had three daughters and one son live to maturity.

Peggy Taylor was a reluctant and, for the most part, reclusive first lady. She delegated her social responsibilities to her daughter, Elizabeth Taylor Bliss. Because Mrs. Taylor was never seen in public, rumors circulated that she was purposely kept hidden due to her rough frontier habits—it was said around Washington that the wife of the president had no manners and was even known to smoke a pipe. The truth is she was a well-educated, well-traveled woman who simply resented the sacrifice of her retirement years with her husband to the office of the presidency. She had little interest in superficial socializing and little inclination to conform to public expectations solely for the sake of appearances.

Mrs. Taylor's predictions about the toll of the presidency on her husband proved correct in 1850 when he died suddenly after completing less than half of his term. Margaret Taylor died two years later, on August 18, 1852. After a long life of hard work and sacrifice, the role of first lady proved a difficult final chapter for Peggy Taylor.

ABIGAIL POWERS FILLMORE
1798–1853
MILLARD FILLMORE ADMINISTRATION 1850–1853

Twenty-year-old Abigail Powers, a well-educated young woman who was passionate about books and reading, took a teaching job in the year 1818 in a small town in upstate New York. Miss Powers hoped her income would help support her family after the sudden death of her father. One of her students was a young man named Millard Fillmore. Romance soon blossomed between the teacher and her student, and in February of 1826 they were married. A quarter of a century later, that young man would be president of the United States and his teacher would be first lady.

Tall, fair-skinned Abigail Powers Fillmore, named for another first lady, Abigail Adams, was born in 1798 in the Finger Lakes region of New York. Her marriage to Millard Fillmore was a happy one; together they had a daughter and a son. During the many separations made necessary by his career, the Fillmores exchanged volumes of letters in which they discussed matters both personal and political. Millard Fillmore

began to look to his wife as one of his most trusted advisors, a habit that would remain with him in the White House. Abigail Fillmore was a bright woman with an active and curious mind. Although she gave up teaching after the birth of her first child, she never lost her love of learning. As an adult, she taught herself French and learned to play the piano.

In the White House, Mrs. Fillmore remained true to her interest in education and delegated much of her social responsibility to her daughter, Abby. Her proudest accomplishment as first lady was the White House library. Mrs. Fillmore lobbied for the funds and then personally selected and gathered the volumes for the first permanent library in the president's house. Her library drew an impressive list of visitors to the White House, including Charles Dickens, Washington Irving, and William Makepeace Thackeray. Mrs. Fillmore also believed strongly in the cause of abolition, and she worked hard to convince her husband not to sign the Fugitive Slave Act, which required free states to return escaped slaves to those who claimed them in the slaveholding states. Millard Fillmore confidently relied upon his wife's advice; although she was not the public, outspoken advisor that Sarah Polk had been, Abigail had strong beliefs and had a husband ready to give them a hearing.

Abigail Fillmore was the first president's wife to attend the inauguration of her husband's successor, and it was at the ceremony for incoming president Franklin Pierce that she contracted the bronchial illness that led to her death only weeks later. Abigail Powers Fillmore left her husband, two children, and an enduring legacy, best described in a newspaper notice of her death that called her "a lady of great strength of mind, dignified manners, genteel deportment, and of much energy of character."

Abigail Fillmore was a unique first lady. She was the first to have grown up in poverty and the first to have worked to support herself as an adult. In a break with the prevailing tradition of the day, she continued to work as a teacher after her marriage and gave up her position only after the birth of her first child. She was her husband's most influential advisor, and her humanitarianism had a profound effect on his decisions as president.

JANE MEANS APPLETON PIERCE
1806–1863
FRANKLIN PIERCE ADMINISTRATION 1853–1857

One observer at a New Year's reception at the Pierce White House remarked that Jane Pierce was "the very picture of melancholy." No description could have been more apt. For Jane Means Appleton Pierce, wife of fourteenth president Franklin Pierce, the White House held only sadness; her years there were a struggle with intensely personal grief in a very public setting.

Jane Pierce, born in Hampton, New Hampshire, in 1806 into two of New England's most prominent families, had always preferred private life with her family to the public life her husband's political career required. Franklin Pierce was not insensitive to his wife's preferences—he resigned his United States Senate seat in 1842 so that he could return his family to the quiet of a law practice in New Hampshire—but his own desires to serve his state and later his country often outweighed his loyalty to his wife's preferences. Pierce had promised Jane that he would not seek the nomination for the presidency in 1852, but when his party called, he accepted.

For Jane Pierce, the already unpleasant prospect of returning to Washington after her husband's unexpected election to the presidency became truly unbearable when her last surviving son, Benjamin, was killed in a train accident only two months before his father's inauguration. Jane and Franklin's first son had died as an infant, their second at the age of four. The loss of Bennie was simply too much for Jane to bear. In Washington, while Franklin distracted himself from his sadness with the work of holding together a nation on the verge of civil war, Jane Pierce retreated into a private world of grief and spent her days in the family quarters of the White House writing letters to her deceased son. Her aunt and close friend, Abby Kent Means, traveled with the Pierces to Washington to serve as official hostess.

For the first half of her husband's term in office, Jane Pierce did not appear in public. In the next two years, Jane did occasionally appear, but she never truly emerged from her grief. The one thing that seemed to direct her attention away from her sadness was her increasing work for the cause of abolition. Unfortunately, this cause put her at odds with her own husband, who still clung to the belief that the Union could survive half-slave and half-free and refused to support the end of slavery.

The Pierces left Washington in 1857, both worn down by their personal and professional trials. Jane Pierce lived another six years before succumbing to tuberculosis in 1863. Franklin Pierce, weakened by a long struggle with alcohol and harassed by a public who would not forgive him for failing to support the Union in the Civil War, died six years later. They are buried side by side in the Old North Cemetery in Concord, New Hampshire.

Jane Pierce would have preferred life in her family's home in Concord, New Hampshire, pictured at left, to life in the White House. But like so many women of her day, she followed the path of her husband and dutifully traveled to Washington to become first lady. After Franklin Pierce's difficult presidency and the tragic deaths of her three sons, however, even their home in New Hampshire could not offer Jane Pierce the peace and security she sought.

For Jane Pierce, the White House was the scene of her deepest mourning; the elegance was overshadowed by her sadness. She is pictured above with the last of her three sons, Bennie, who was killed in a railroad accident; Jane Pierce never recovered from her deep grief. As the shadow of civil war loomed ever darker on the horizon, the Pierce years were difficult for the nation as well as the first family.

HARRIET LANE

1830–1903

JAMES BUCHANAN ADMINISTRATION 1857–1861

As a young man, James Buchanan was engaged to be married to a woman named Anne Coleman. After a quarrel, however, Miss Coleman left Buchanan and went to visit friends. A short time later she died—perhaps by suicide. James Buchanan, stricken by grief and remorse, remained a bachelor for the remainder of his life. As the only president to enter and leave the White House a single man, he did, however, have the support and devotion of a beautiful, spirited, young niece who, as official White House hostess, won the hearts of the American people.

Eleven-year-old Harriet Lane came to live with her uncle James at his Wheatland estate in Pennsylvania after the loss of both her parents. At Wheatland, and later in London, where her uncle served as ambassador, Harriet received a broad education, both in academic subjects and in the art of entertaining. James Buchanan included his niece in all that he did. He discussed his career, his politics, and his ambitions, and he made her privy to discussions with the many prominent guests who passed through his home. In London, Harriet became friends with Queen Victoria and her family. By the time Uncle James was elected to the presidency in 1856, Harriet Lane, at the age of twenty-six, was well prepared to take over the full range of social duties that traditionally fell to the first lady.

The Buchanan White House took on an elegant, almost royal feel under the influence of young Harriet. Her receptions were exquisite and very formal; her dresses were the absolute height of current fashion. Her preference for wide, lacy collars and full, stiff skirts soon dictated fashion across America. After the dark years of the Pierce administration, young, beautiful, vivacious Harriet Lane was received by Washington as a welcome breath of spring.

But all was not rosy at the Buchanan White House. The threat of civil war loomed darkly overhead, and tensions between northerners and southerners in the capital flared. While the president and his niece were Pennsylvanians, they counted southerners among their closest friends. Harriet tried to keep White House receptions free of the great tensions that were tearing at the country, but in the end, her uncle's presidency fell victim to the civil strife that would soon lead to war.

Harriet Lane—a first lady in the eyes of the American people if not by definition—was a true celebrity and a woman whose humanitarianism and sense of culture were a credit to the role. At a difficult time in American history, as the country moved each day closer to civil war, she brought life and spirit to the city of Washington. She also left a lasting legacy of social service. Passionate about art, Harriet Lane began the practice of inviting accomplished artists to the White House; and she lobbied hard for the establishment of a national gallery of art, to which she eventually donated her own extensive private collection of paintings. Miss Lane also established the first White House greenhouse. Perhaps her most impressive accomplishment, however, was her work on behalf of the Native American. Harriet Lane took up the cause of Native American welfare at a time when few Americans considered it a cause worthy of their attention. After leaving the White House, Harriet Lane did eventually marry, but her life was scarred by the loss of two young sons and her husband. She died in 1903.

Harriet Lane considered America's treatment of Native Americans unjust and inhumane. Her interest in Native American culture grew out of her study and collection of Indian art; Miss Lane was one of the first to collect the art of America's indigenous peoples. Later, she became the Indians' most outspoken advocate in Washington; the gratitude of many Native Americans was expressed by the popularity of "Harriet" as a name for Indian children of the mid-nineteenth century.

MARY TODD LINCOLN
1818–1882
ABRAHAM LINCOLN ADMINISTRATION 1861–1865

Perhaps no first lady suffered so much in the role as did Mary Lincoln, wife of President Abraham Lincoln. Mrs. Lincoln came to the White House full of hope, but tortured by insecurities. Eventually, she would lose a son, her husband, and her sanity.

Mary Todd was the bright, witty daughter of one of the most influential and wealthy families in Kentucky. She was born on December 14, 1818, and as a young girl received an education that included, besides the basic subjects, French, music, and drama. She grew up with a great love of politics, and it was this common interest that drew her to the rugged, self-educated Abraham Lincoln when the two met in Springfield, Illinois. Despite the objections of her family, who recognized no great potential in Mr. Lincoln, Abraham and Mary were married on November 4, 1842.

Although the Lincolns were of opposite temperaments, they had a close, devoted marriage and together doted upon their three sons. Opinionated and outspoken, Mary always maintained an active interest in her husband's career, and from the start she had complete confidence in his abilities. When he ran for the presidency in 1860, Mary assumed a leading role in his victorious campaign. She followed him on the road and gave her own interviews to journalists. The victory was as satisfying to Mary as it was to her husband. Nonetheless, the prospect of moving to Washington filled Mrs. Lincoln with equal measures of anticipation and dread. She was confident in her husband's ability to lead and excited about her own role, but she was worried that as "westerners" they would not be accepted by Washington society. Abe, though possessed of a brilliant mind, was never very polished, and she, while at home in the most elegant homes of Illinois and Kentucky, was uncertain of how she would be received by the leaders of Washington society.

In the White House, Mary Lincoln's insecurities soon got the best of her. She dressed extravagantly and redecorated the White House with a flourish of spending that exceeded her budget by seven thousand dollars. Her clothes, always the finest that money could buy, were garish and overstated. The press observed Mrs. Lincoln's every move, her every purchase, her every new gown. Under such scrutiny, her insecurities multiplied—the more they wrote, the more she spent; the more they criticized, the harder she tried. She went on wild spending sprees and ran up huge debts all over Washington. To make matters worse, the headaches that had always bothered her became worse than ever. She was confined to bed for days at a time, and she experienced violent mood swings—one day she was lavishly entertaining at huge White House receptions; the next day she was back in bed and complaining of terrible headaches.

When the Civil War began, Mary's troubles multiplied. Her loyalties to the Union were questioned in the press due to the fact that she had a brother and three half-brothers fighting for the Confederacy. And when her dear son Willie died of typhoid fever, she was criticized again, this time for wallowing in her own grief when thousands of American mothers were losing their own sons to the war.

Through all her troubles, however, Mary Lincoln enjoyed the support and affection of her husband, who, although often exasperated by her excesses and mood swings, remained loyal and always sought her advice and opinions. Mary Lincoln remained very involved in her husband's politics. Despite the accusations of southern sympathies, Mary Lincoln was devoted to achieving freedom for the black men, women, and children of America. During the war she also regularly visited wounded soldiers and donated and raised money to support widows and orphans.

Despite the positives, Mary Lincoln was already sinking under the weight of her role when Abraham Lincoln was assassinated on April 14, 1865. The war had ended, but for Mary the tragedy continued. Overcome with grief, she remained in the White House as her husband was buried and then transported back by train to Illinois. While she remained secluded upstairs, the White House was looted and ransacked by mobs of angry citizens. Mrs. Lincoln eventually returned to Illinois but lived the remainder of her life in poor health. She died on July 16, 1882.

Mary Lincoln's great unrecognized achievement was her support of the abolition movement and her partnership with her husband in the Emancipation Proclamation. Perhaps because she had grown up in the slaveholding South and seen the inhumanity of slavery firsthand, Mary Lincoln was a passionate abolitionist. She quietly raised funds for abolitionist causes and was the first president's wife to invite black Americans to the White House as guests of her family. When Abraham Lincoln signed the Emancipation Proclamation on January 1, 1863, it was in large part thanks to his wife's insistence. Mary Lincoln called the end of slavery the end of "the great evil, that has been so long allowed to curse the land."

This lithograph portrays the Lincoln family at home after the death of their second son, Willie. Robert, the first-born, dropped out of Harvard Law School to join the Union army during the Civil War. He later completed his studies and worked as a lawyer in Illinois. Tad, the Lincoln's youngest son, died at the age of eighteen. It was Robert Lincoln who took on responsibility for his ailing mother in the years following Abraham Lincoln's assassination.

ELIZA MCCARDLE JOHNSON
1810–1876
ANDREW JOHNSON ADMINISTRATION 1865–1869

After the devastation of the Civil War and the great tragedy of the assassination of President Lincoln, the nation was worn out, deeply divided, and somber. The White House itself had been nearly destroyed by the mobs that had run through its rooms while Mary Lincoln grieved her husband upstairs. The difficult task of leading the troubled nation fell to Andrew Johnson of Tennessee, and the title of first lady fell to his wife of nearly forty years, Eliza McCardle Johnson.

Eliza was sixteen years old when she married eighteen-year-old Andrew Johnson in Greeneville, Tennessee. Theirs was a unique and close relationship. Andrew Johnson was illiterate when he met Eliza; with her help, he learned to read and to write and began his life of public service. The Johnsons had two daughters and three sons. Throughout most of Andrew's career, which included terms in Washington as a United States representative and a senator, Mrs. Johnson remained in Tennessee, preferring her simple life there with the children to the more public life in the nation's capital. When the Civil War began, the Johnson's found themselves in the difficult position of being Union supporters in a southern state. When Andrew was appointed military governor of Tennessee, Eliza spent several treacherous weeks traveling in secret through the Tennessee countryside to reach the safety of her husband's protection in Nashville. When Abraham Lincoln selected Andrew Johnson to be his vice-presidential running mate in 1864, Mrs. Johnson again remained in Tennessee; only when her husband ascended to the presidency upon Lincoln's assassination did she finally agree to move to Washington.

As first lady, Eliza Johnson willingly handed all social duties over to her daughter, Martha Patterson, and retired to the family quarters. Mrs. Johnson was weak with tuberculosis and seeking some peace amid the turmoil of post-Civil War Washington. She was a gentle, unpretentious woman who was beloved by her staff and servants. She once said that she and Andrew were "two souls and minds merged into one," and their close relationship continued as he struggled under the weight of a very difficult presidency. Eliza made only two public appearances during her White House years, one at a reception for Queen Emma of the Sandwich Islands and the other at a family birthday party.

Martha Patterson filled in admirably for her mother. She was well-educated, for she had studied at Georgetown and spent many years in Washington with her father. She was a sensible and frugal woman who managed the refurbishing of the White House on a tight budget and even kept cows on the lawn to provide milk for the family. Martha Patterson was quite capable of fulfilling her social duties, but she nonetheless remarked to reporters, "We are plain people from the mountains of Tennessee called here for a short time by a national calamity. I trust not too much will be expected of us."

When Andrew Johnson's difficult term ended, the family gladly returned to Tennessee, where they were received as great heroes, a turnaround from the not so distant days when they had lived in hiding due to their Union loyalties. Mrs. Johnson died in 1876, six months after the death of her husband. Both are buried in the town where they met, Greeneville, Tennessee.

Eliza McCardle Johnson was born in Leesburg, Tennessee, on October 4, 1810. An only child, she lost her father at a young age and was raised by her mother. Only sixteen at the time of her marriage to Andrew Johnson, Eliza not only took on responsibility for raising a family, but also became her husband's private tutor. Through a devoted course of patient instruction, Eliza raised her husband out of illiteracy and set him on the path toward the presidency.

Julia Grant, pictured at left, was born in St. Louis, Missouri, in 1826. The ruins of her birthplace are pictured below. She and Ulysses Grant enjoyed a long and happy marriage. They were parents to three sons and a daughter and were approaching their sixtieth wedding anniversary when Ulysses died in 1885. So eager was Mrs. Grant for her husband to become the president that Mr. Grant is said to have remarked to her upon completing the oath of office at his inauguration, "My dear, I hope you are satisfied."

JULIA BOGGS DENT GRANT
1826–1902
ULYSSES S. GRANT ADMINISTRATION 1869–1877

Perhaps no first lady before her so thoroughly enjoyed her time in the White House as did Julia Grant, wife of President and war hero Ulysses S. Grant. She once called her years as first lady "a bright and beautiful dream." An energetic and driven woman, Mrs. Grant was both a gracious and polished hostess and an informed, intelligent advisor who exercised a powerful, behind-the-scenes influence on her husband.

The daughter of a wealthy slaveholding planter, twenty-two-year-old Julia Boggs Dent went against her parents' wishes when she married Ulysses S. Grant on August 22, 1848. The Dents, although they allowed the marriage ceremony to take place in their home, saw little promise in Mr. Grant and little chance of happiness for their daughter with a career military man. But if the Dents were less than thrilled with the match, the Grants were absolutely opposed. The groom's parents did not attend their son's wedding, for they were unable to accept his marriage into a slaveholding family. Despite the great odds against them, Julia and Ulysses built a happy, close, and affectionate union.

In the early years of their marriage, Julia followed Ulysses from fort to fort as he progressed in his military career. By 1852, however, she was in weakened health and remained at home in St. Louis while her husband went to California. Two years later, Grant retired from the army and returned to his wife and children. He seemed to be putting the military life forever behind him.

The Civil War, of course, changed the course of the Grants' lives forever. With the outbreak of the war, Ulysses was appointed to command a volunteer regiment and eventually rose to be commander of the Union army. During the war, Julia stayed with her husband in camp whenever she could and sent him volumes of letters when they were separated. As General Grant's fame grew, Mrs. Grant began to fill with ambition for her husband, and herself. During the war, she met Mrs. Lincoln at the White House. From that point on, Julia felt certain that she and Ulysses

and their four children would one day make the president's house their home.

On a wave of post-war popularity, and with the full and enthusiastic support of his wife, Ulysses S. Grant was elected president in 1868.

The disappointment felt by many first ladies—both those who never wanted any part of the role and those who had looked forward to it with anticipation—was not to be the lot of Julia Grant. Despite the scandals that rocked her husband's two administrations, and his general inefficacy as president, Julia Grant enjoyed every day of her White House stay. Her first project was an extensive and expensive remodeling job. The new Grant White House was extravagant. Some said it was gaudy—the perfect setting for the lavish entertaining of the Grants. It is reported that the average formal dinner at the Grant White House ran up a bill close to one thousand dollars. For special occasions, the cost nearly doubled. Julia Grant relished and encouraged the spotlight that now shone almost continually on the first lady. She kept herself well informed on her husband's politics and is said to have wielded great influence over his decisions. But although she had shown a growing interest in women's rights and the suffrage movement, as first lady, Julia Grant played to perfection the role of the good wife. She concerned herself for the most part with social matters, and she was always careful to keep her political interests and influence from the public eye. Perhaps her most cherished moment in the White House was the wedding of Nellie, the Grants' only daughter. Like everything else that Julia Grant ever did in the White House, the wedding was a grand, lavish, and memorable affair.

When Ulysses Grant left office in 1877, his wife followed reluctantly. For Julia Grant, the White House had been everything she had ever dreamed. In retirement, Julia traveled around the world with her husband and young son, Jesse. After Ulysses' death, Julia lived in New York City. She died in 1902 and is buried beside her husband in Grant's Tomb overlooking the Hudson River.

LUCY WEBB HAYES
1831–1889
RUTHERFORD B. HAYES ADMINISTRATION 1877–1881

Born in August of 1831 in Chillicothe, Ohio, Lucy Hayes was the first of the first ladies to hold a college degree. She was also the first to have the use of the telephone and typewriter. Her days in the White House saw the installation of the first permanent running water system, and her every move and every word was reported closely by a suddenly large corps of female journalists whose sole responsibility was to report on the first lady. America had changed immeasurably since the days of Martha Washington and Abigail Adams; Lucy Hayes had the education, resources, and opportunity to make the role of first lady an active, independent, and powerful one. Instead, she chose to focus on her family responsibilities and, for the most part, leave the spotlight to her husband, President Rutherford B. Hayes.

After the departure of Julia Grant, who had lived in the White House for eight years, speculation abounded about the woman who would take her place. As the Ohio governor's wife, Mrs. Hayes had lent her voice to many public causes—reforming the state's mental institutions, dealing with the care of war orphans, improving public education—and she was known to have been a passionate abolitionist before the war and a supporter of the temperance movement. Washington expected an activist first lady; what they got instead was a serious-minded, reserved, intelligent woman who from the first was determined to keep her name from becoming too closely associated with any one cause.

Lucy Hayes, with the support of her husband, immediately established a White House policy banning alcohol at all receptions. Mocked in the press as "Lemonade Lucy," Mrs. Hayes stuck to her guns but also resisted efforts by the temperance movement to enlist her leadership. For Mrs. Hayes, it was a private issue. Entertaining at the Hayes White House was simple and sedate, with the most memorable occasions being family celebrations of birthdays and weddings

and a ceremony in which the Hayeses renewed their wedding vows on their twenty-fifth anniversary. At public receptions, Mrs. Hayes began a tradition of having the Marine Corps Band break into "Home, Sweet Home" precisely at ten o'clock as a signal to all in attendance that it was time to leave. Again, this brought criticism in the press; but for Lucy Hayes, the White House was first and foremost the family home, and she was not an elected official, but a wife and mother. This attitude was a disappointment to women's rights groups who had looked to their new, educated first lady as a potential leader; but Mrs. Hayes always seemed untouched by public perceptions and criticisms. She was comfortable with her lifestyle and confident that her choices were the right ones.

Lucy Hayes did not totally shun public duties. She was the first president's wife to travel without of her husband and to deliver prepared speeches, a part of the job that is now considered a requirement for first ladies. She also took an active role in her family's Methodist church and served as president of the Women's Missionary Society.

Lucy Webb Hayes, who is commemorated in a portrait commissioned by the Women's Christian Temperance Union that hangs in the White House today, died in 1889. She is buried alongside her husband at their home in Fremont, Ohio.

First Lady Lucy Hayes wielded a powerful influence over her husband the president. So widely recognized was her power that when Mrs. Hayes left Washington for a brief time during the Hayes administration, a reporter remarked that Rutherford B. Hayes would "during the absence of Mrs. Hayes serve as acting president." President Hayes was unperturbed by such references to his wife's influence—he was, in fact, quite open about his dependence upon her for advice. Nonetheless, Lucy Hayes was never an activist first lady; she always maintained a firm belief that hers was essentially a private role in a public setting, and she resisted the temptation to become too closely aligned with any cause or issue.

LUCRETIA RUDOLPH GARFIELD
1832–1918
JAMES GARFIELD ADMINISTRATION 1881

Lucretia Rudolph Garfield, born in Hiram, Ohio, in 1832, came to the role of first lady in 1881 with confidence and great ambition. Crete, as her husband President James Garfield called her, was an independent, well-educated woman who read Greek and Latin and spoke fluent German and French; and she had more than parties and entertaining on her mind as she settled in Washington. Mrs. Garfield envisioned a White House busy with visits from accomplished artists and authors and a personal schedule that put her position and notoriety to work for educational and cultural causes. As a special project, Mrs. Garfield planned a detailed course of research dedicated to the historical restoration of each room in the White House. For Crete Garfield, the potential of the role of first lady appeared unlimited.

Unfortunately, Mrs. Garfield's plans were cut short—first by the malaria that struck her just months into her husband's term and then by the assassination of the president in July of 1881. During his wife's illness, President Garfield put her needs above all else. He arranged for her to recuperate on the New Jersey shore and was on his way to visit her there when he was shot by a disgruntled office seeker named Charles Guiteau. Learning of the attack, Crete Garfield forgot her own health and returned to the White House immediately to nurse her dying husband; for two months she stood by his side night and day. One observer remarked that the first lady was "firm and quiet and full of purpose. . . ." Her devotion became the talk of the American people, but it was not enough. James Garfield died in September of 1881.

Crete Garfield might have been a memorable and influential first lady. She and James, who met while students at the Eclectic Institute in Ohio, had a close marriage, one that had emerged strongly from some early difficulties. The values of Crete and James Garfield were reflected in the lives of their children, all of whom made education and achievement a priority in their lives. As children, the young Garfields learned the classics at their mother's side. All four of the Garfield sons attended their father's alma mater, Williams College in Massachusetts, and three went on from there to law school. Harry, the eldest, served as president of Williams College and, during World War I, earned the Distinguished Service Medal for his work in the U.S. Food Administration. James, his father's namesake, served as secretary of the interior during the Theodore Roosevelt administration; and youngest son, Abram, attended Massachusetts Institute of Technology after graduating from Williams and became an accomplished architect. The Garfields' only daughter, Mary, attended private schools in Ohio and Connecticut before her marriage.

On the campaign trail and in the White House, the Garfields were truly partners. Crete was a shrewd and forceful spokesperson for her husband. She gave interviews to the press, discussed politics with her husband's contemporaries, and in almost two decades in Washington—while James served as a United States representative—Crete Garfield earned a reputation for being strong-minded and intelligent. Her husband called her "unstampedable," a tribute to her strong convictions and unquestionable grace and discretion in public. Mrs. Garfield believed in the equality of women, but decried activism and extremism. To her mind, equality was best proven by actions—thus her devotion to her project of the White House restoration and her disdain for the purely superficial and social duties of the first lady. Lucretia Garfield had great plans to define the first lady as a cultural, as well as social, leader, but she never got a chance to fulfill her potential. She died in 1918 and is buried beside her husband.

Like so many first ladies before and after her, Crete Garfield was awed by the history of the White House. She felt herself living there "among the shadows of the last eighty years" and quickly became devoted to her project of a historically accurate restoration. This project was part of Mrs. Garfield's overall efforts to make the role of first lady a full time job. She frequently traveled with her husband and joined him at public appearances beyond the purely social. Mrs. Garfield had compiled a list of the leading artists and authors of the day with intentions of inviting each one to the White House for a dinner or reception. In short, Mrs. Garfield, after years as the devoted wife and selfless mother, hoped to find an outlet for her creative and intellectual energies.

ELLEN LEWIS HERNDON ARTHUR

1837–1880

CHESTER A. ARTHUR ADMINISTRATION 1881–1885

While living in the White House as the twenty-first president, Chester A. Arthur had fresh flowers placed each day beneath the portrait of his wife, Nell, who had passed away a little more than a year before he took the oath of office. President Arthur's devotion to his late wife remained unshaken during his White House years. "Honors to me now," he remarked after her death, "are not what they once were." Although his sister, Mary Arthur McElroy, often fulfilled the social duties that normally fell to the first lady, out of respect for the memory of his wife, President Arthur never bestowed upon anyone the title of official White House hostess.

Ellen Lewis Herndon was born in Culpeper Court House, Virginia, on August 30, 1837. Known as Nell, she met Chester Arthur in New York City in 1856 and married him three years later on October 25, 1859. Nell, a true southern gentlewoman with great political and social ambitions, was an accomplished soprano who sang with the Mendelsohn Glee Club in New York City. The Arthurs had two sons and a daughter together—one son died as a child—and by most accounts had a happy, stable marriage. Although there is evidence that during the Civil War tensions developed over Mrs. Arthur's private support of the Confederacy. With many relatives serving in the southern army and her old Virginia loyalties still strong within her, Mrs. Arthur likely was very torn between her old family loyalties and her adult ties.

It was after a concert with the Mendelsohn Glee Club on a cold January night that Mrs. Arthur first took ill with what would soon develop into pneumonia. She died only days later, on January 12, 1880. Nell Arthur was buried at the Arthur family plot in Rural Cemetery in Albany, New York. She was joined less than six years later by her husband, the former president.

Nell and Chester Arthur had two children who lived to maturity, a son and a daughter, both named after their parents. Son Chester was born in 1864. Daughter Nell, pictured at left, was born in 1871 and was only nine years old when she lost her mother. In the White House, her father saw that her privacy was carefully guarded and that she was shielded from the inquiring eyes of the public.

Nell Arthur would have thoroughly enjoyed life as first lady had she lived long enough to join her husband in the White House. She was familiar with Washington since she spent much of her childhood in the city. She had on two occasions even visited the White House, once as a guest at the second inauguration of Abraham Lincoln and a second time at the wedding of President and Mrs. Grant's daughter, Nellie. Nell Arthur was a gracious entertainer and was skilled at the art of social persuasion; she enjoyed the role that her social duties played in the advancement of her husband's career.

Mrs. Arthur also had early experience in the spotlight. As a child, she and her family gained national attention when her father—a navy officer—heroically evacuated his passengers before going down with his ship during a storm off Cape Hatteras.

FRANCES FOLSOM CLEVELAND

1864–1947

GROVER CLEVELAND ADMINISTRATIONS 1885–1889, 1893–1897

After the tragedy of the Garfield assassination and the lonely widower days of President Arthur, it was with great anticipation and excitement that Americans greeted the news that their new president, Grover Cleveland, a bachelor when elected, was to be married. The new first lady—a twenty-one-year-old named Frances Folsom—met or exceeded all public expectations. The youngest first lady in history, Frances, or Frankie as she was soon known, was charming, witty, bright, and unaffected; in no time at all she was a true American celebrity.

The wedding of President Grover Cleveland and Frances Folsom was celebrated on June 2, 1886, with a twenty-one gun salute, the music of John Philip Sousa and the Marine Band, and the simultaneous ringing of church bells throughout Washington, D.C. The president was nearly thirty years older than his bride; in fact, he had met his wife as an infant, the daughter of his law partner and friend Oscar Folsom. When Mr. Folsom died, Grover Cleveland took over the administration of his friend's estate and the unofficial guardianship of his eleven-year-old daughter. Grover Cleveland had played an important role in Frances Folsom's life for all of her childhood; now he was to be her husband.

Frances Cleveland was a natural for the role thrust upon her by her marriage to the president; and she filled it with her own unique spirit, charm, and vitality. Bright and attractive, she played the piano, spoke fluent German and French, and had a true compassion for and love of the people of America. Her two regular weekly receptions—one of which she held on Saturday, so that working women could attend—drew great crowds of devoted admirers. Frankie handled the attention and adulation with true grace. She never spoke publicly to the press, but answered the endless volumes of fan mail addressed to her and seemed undaunted by the intense scrutiny focused on every element of her appearance and demeanor.

When Grover Cleveland—defeated at the end of his first term—won reelection after a four year hiatus, he and his wife returned to their beloved White House, where the first lady was faced with a new dimension to her role—motherhood. When Esther—the first child born in the White House itself—joined sister Ruth in 1893, the Clevelands began to worry about the American people's interest in their family and the potential danger to the children. At that point much of the public access to the White House was restricted, and the family spent a great deal of time in their own private residence located elsewhere in Washington. But Frances did not lose the affections of the American people; when the Clevelands moved to Princeton, New Jersey, in 1897, after Grover Cleveland's second term was completed, Frankie Cleveland remained one of the most popular first ladies of all time.

Frances Cleveland did not take up any one cause, nor did she delve too deeply into the political affairs of her husband, although she was aware of the world around her and was a firm believer in education as the key to equality. At a time when many Americans were struggling with unemployment and poverty, Mrs. Cleveland's spirit and energy were an inspiration. Frances lived nearly forty years after the death of her husband in 1908. She remarried in 1913; and during the Great Depression, she again won the hearts of the American people for her work to collect clothing for the poor. Frances Folsom Cleveland Preston died on October 29, 1947, in Baltimore. She is buried beside the former president in Princeton, New Jersey.

Frances Folsom was born in Buffalo, New York, on July 21, 1864. She knew Grover Cleveland all of her life as a friend and advisor, but it was while she was attending Wells College in Aurora, New York, that their relationship became romantic. They were engaged in August of 1885, but kept their plans secret until five days before their wedding the following June. Rumors were rampant in Washington, however, in the months leading up to the first-ever White House wedding ceremony. The press reported that the president was to marry Emma Folsom, Frances's mother; Cleveland added to the speculation by neither confirming nor denying the rumors. When Frances's identity was finally revealed, all the president's best attempts at maintaining her privacy went for naught; the media circus that would characterize Mrs. Cleveland's entire stay in Washington began in full force. Our youngest first lady is pictured at right in a photo taken in 1886.

43

CAROLINE SCOTT HARRISON

1832–1892

BENJAMIN HARRISON ADMINISTRATION
1889–1893

Caroline Scott Harrison and her husband, the twenty-third president, Benjamin Harrison, were disparagingly called "homebodies" by many in the press who believed that the couple did not have the sophistication or the social polish to be the "first family" of the United States. Mrs. Harrison, old-fashioned in her beliefs and devoted to the roles of wife and mother, was, however, far from the simple woman that the public perceived.

Caroline Scott was born in Ohio in 1832. She met Benjamin Harrison while he was a student at Farmers College, where her father was a professor. They put their marriage on hold while both pursued an education, he at law school and she at the Oxford Female Institute in Oxford, Ohio, where she studied French and music. After their marriage in 1853, the Harrisons lived in Indiana and Ohio while Benjamin practiced law and began his involvement in politics and Caroline took over the responsibility for raising their son and daughter. In 1881, when Benjamin was elected to the United States Senate, the Harrisons moved to Washington.

Eight years later, Benjamin was elected to the presidency and Caroline moved her family—daughter Mary McKee, daughter-in-law May Saunders Harrison, three grandchildren, father, sister Elizabeth Lord, and widowed daughter Mary Lord Dimmick—into the White House. Like so many occupants of the president's house before them, the Harrisons found the building in need of repair and improvement; and Caroline set about a determined course of modernization. Her first plan involved a complete rebuilding of the house, but she had to settle eventually for money to "clean up" the existing house. Mrs. Harrison had new floors installed, got rid of the long time resident insect and rodent populations, chose new wallpaper and paint, ordered new bathrooms installed, and, despite her own fears about safety, agreed to the installation of electricity. The "magic lights," as Mrs. Harrison called them, always made her uncomfortable, and she never once touched the switch to turn them on and off. She often left them burning all night until the staff returned in the morning to turn them off. Mrs. Harrison, a skilled china-painter who gave lessons in the art at the

The Daughters of the American Revolution (DAR) was founded after the Sons of the American Revolution denied women access to their organization. Mrs. Harrison accepted the position of president general of the organization in hopes of helping the members recognize the achievements of women in the past and open avenues of power and influence to women of the present and future. In a speech delivered by the first lady to the women of the DAR, she lauded the contributions of the women of colonial America and found inspiration in their accomplishments for the women of her day: "The unselfish part they acted constantly commands itself to our admiration and example."

White House, also designed a new set of official presidential china, and it was at her suggestion that the first White House Christmas tree was erected and decorated. One of the great discoveries made during her extensive renovations was a desk once presented to President Hayes by Queen Victoria of England. The desk was used by President Benjamin Harrison and was put to use once more by President John F. Kennedy almost a century later.

Mrs. Harrison was, as her critics charged, a "homebody." She was old-fashioned and motherly and domestic. But she was also an independent and intelligent woman who was confident in her priorities and determined to fulfill her duties. She served as the first president general of the Daughters of the American Revolution, supported the Women's Medical Fund at Johns Hopkins University, which gave assistance to female students, and was also a trusted advisor to her husband. Most importantly, she was a woman comfortable with her own role, able to balance the demands and joys of her private life with those of her public life and to live satisfied with the results. Caroline Harrison died in the White House in 1892, two weeks before her husband lost his bid for reelection.

IDA SAXTON MCKINLEY
1847–1907
WILLIAM MCKINLEY ADMINISTRATION 1897–1901

President William McKinley's last words, spoken to his secretary moments after an assassin's bullet pierced his abdomen, were: "My wife—be careful how you tell her! Oh, be careful!" These words are evidence of President McKinley's undying devotion to his wife, Ida Saxton McKinley, a woman who, as first lady, suffered great personal hardship and remained for the most part a mystery to the American public.

Ida Saxton was born in Canton, Ohio, in January of 1847. She grew up in great wealth and privilege and attended the prestigious Brook Hall Seminary finishing school. Her father was a prominent banker who, believing that women should understand and control their own finances, taught his daughter the business of banking and personal finance and employed her in his own bank. When she met William McKinley in 1867, Ida Saxton was a refined, charming, and attractive young girl full of life and great promise. Ida and William married on January 25, 1871, in Canton and looked forward to a life of great joy.

Within four years, however, tragedy struck three times. Ida's mother and two infant daughters died in short succession; Mrs. McKinley was left distraught and inconsolable. She never had another child and shortly thereafter began experiencing terrible, undiagnosed seizures. William McKinley did his best to comfort his wife, but Ida fell into a depression from which she would never truly emerge. By the time William sought the presidency in 1896, Ida rarely left their home.

In the White House, Mrs. McKinley, while not truly an invalid, was entirely dependent upon her husband, who worked hard to balance the responsibilities of the presidency with the needs of his wife. The two were rarely separated for more than a few hours, and Mrs. McKinley was often present during his meetings and private political discussions. Due to her seizures, which could strike at any time, President McKinley broke normal protocol and had his wife seated at his side during state dinners. If a seizure began, he simply and quietly covered her face with his handkerchief until it passed, and then they both continued on as if

In his bid for the presidency in 1896, William McKinley ran what was referred to as a "Front Porch" campaign, in which he gave speeches from his home rather than traveling the country to reach the voters. At the time, his strategy was considered politically motivated, but it is likely that he remained close to home due to his wife's dependence upon him. As he would throughout his presidency, William McKinley made his wife's comfort and care a priority above almost all else.

nothing out of the ordinary had happened. Mrs. McKinley also insisted on participating in receiving lines, and her husband arranged for her to be seated while she went through the motions of greeting each visitor. Mrs. McKinley never agreed to relinquish her official duties, and she used her own substantial private income to dress elegantly. She therefore held on to at least the pretense of being the social leader of the White House, although Edith Roosevelt, the wife of Vice-President Theodore Roosevelt, often filled in. As a result, the McKinley White House was quiet and somber, and rumors about Mrs. McKinley's condition were rampant.

Ida McKinley withstood much criticism for her reclusiveness and dependence upon her husband, and he suffered in the minds of many who thought his devotion to his wife bordered on the absurd. Historians have since concluded that Ida McKinley suffered from epilepsy, a disease little understood in her day, but which would account for her poor health and bizarre behavior. Mrs. McKinley's health only worsened after the assassination. She died in 1907 and is buried next to the former president in Canton, Ohio.

EDITH KERMIT CAROW ROOSEVELT
1861–1948
THEODORE ROOSEVELT ADMINISTRATION 1901–1909

One of Theodore Roosevelt's close aides once remarked that Edith Roosevelt had spent eight years as first lady "without making a mistake." Her many admirers would heartily agree. As America entered a new century and took on a new international status, and as the role of women in American society continued to broaden and evolve, the position of first lady became more demanding and more visible than ever before. Edith Roosevelt took on the role with confidence and struck a perfect balance between her full, challenging, and active private life and the demands of her public role.

Edith Roosevelt was born Edith Kermit Carow in Norwich, Connecticut, in August of 1861. She and Theodore Roosevelt were close childhood playmates, drawn together by their love of books, nature, and athletics, but lost touch when Theodore entered Harvard. After the sudden death of Roosevelt's first wife, he and Edith renewed their friendship and decided to make a life together. They were married in December of 1886.

As first lady, Edith Roosevelt was expected to present an image suitable to the United States' emerging role as a world leader. Never concerned with fashion or frivolity, Edith Roosevelt was, nonetheless, the model of dignity and grace in all her public appearances. Her years as first lady saw the role evolve into a more official, institutionalized one; and she was the first to have her own private staff, paid for by the government. As the wife of the irrepressible Theodore Roosevelt, mother to five active children ranging in age from toddlers to teenagers, and stepmother to Theodore's spirited, independent, teenage daughter Alice, Edith Roosevelt had a family life that would challenge even the most devoted of mothers. Aware of the intense public scrutiny under which she and her family lived, Edith tenaciously guarded her own and her family's privacy. Her awareness of the necessary separation between the public and the private lives of the president and his family shows in her renovations to the White House. Mrs. Roosevelt insisted that the family quarters be comfortable, spacious, and distinctly separate from the working areas of the house.

Edith Roosevelt was an active and strong woman who enjoyed her daily walk or ride in every kind of weather. She had a great love for art and literature and brought many of the most talented artists, musicians, and authors to the White House. Her public receptions and dinners were formal and quiet; most of her entertaining focused on the family, the culmination of which was the wedding of her stepdaughter Alice, who had become a national celebrity. Unlike many of her predecessors, Mrs. Roosevelt had no real interest in influencing her husband's policies. She was informed about public affairs and politics, but also recognized that it was her husband, not herself, who had been elected by the people.

Edith Roosevelt lived almost forty years after her two terms as first lady. In that time she traveled extensively around the world and remained devoted to her children and grandchildren. She died in 1948 at the family home in Oyster Bay, Long Island, and is buried there beside Theodore.

The family the Roosevelts brought to the White House in 1901 included their own five children, Theodore, Jr., Kermit, Ethel, Archie, and Quentin. They ranged in age from fourteen to four. Edith also had the difficult task of overseeing the teenage years of her stepdaughter, Alice, the daughter of Roosevelt's first wife, Alice Hathaway Lee Roosevelt. Alice's youth and beauty and spirit made her a national celebrity—and a constant challenge to her stepmother. Theodore Roosevelt himself once remarked, "I can do one of two things, I can be president of the United States, or I can control Alice, I cannot possibly do both." Pictured at left are the Roosevelts and their children.

On the question of women's rights, Edith Roosevelt held the traditional view that a woman's first goal should be marriage and family, but she did express a strong belief in the value of education for both sexes. Her greatest contributions to the position of first lady were the dignity which she imparted to the role and her insistence that the president's family did not forfeit the right to privacy the day they moved into the White House.

HELEN HERRON TAFT
1861–1943
WILLIAM TAFT ADMINISTRATION 1909–1913

For Nellie Taft—born Helen Herron in 1861 in Cincinnati—the dream of becoming first lady began in 1877 at the White House reception in honor of the twenty-fifth wedding anniversary of President Hayes and his wife, Lucy. Sixteen-year-old Nellie, a guest along with her parents, was enthralled by the beauty and elegance of the experience. She vowed to a friend that one day she would return to the White House as first lady. Not long after, Nellie met William Howard Taft, the man who would help her dream come true. In 1886, they were married.

After their marriage, the Tafts settled in Cincinnati where William pursued a career as an attorney, then later a judge and a law school dean, while Nellie took care of their home and their growing family, all the while keeping a close eye on her husband's career. William's dream was to serve on the Supreme Court; but after he won a series of government appointments, first to the Philippines and then as secretary of war, Nellie began to believe that her White House dreams might not be farfetched after all. By the time William Taft's name came up for possible presidential candidacy, Nellie's was a familiar face and a strong voice in Washington politics. She lobbied hard for the support of outgoing president Theodore Roosevelt for her husband's candidacy—despite William's expressed preference for a Supreme Court appointment—and once that was secured, Nellie campaigned perhaps more fervently than the candidate himself. Although William Taft might still have been wishing for that Supreme Court appointment, he was elected twenty-seventh president of the United States in 1908, thanks in great part to the determination and hard work of his wife.

On the day of her husband's inauguration, Nellie Taft let the American people know that she planned an active role in his administration by insisting that she—and not, as was traditional, the outgoing president—be seated at her husband's side for the ride down Pennsylvania Avenue after the ceremonies. Her symbolic gesture did not go unnoticed; from that point on, there would be no middle ground for Nellie Taft. To Americans working for women's rights, Mrs. Taft was a role model. Outspoken and forceful, Nellie Taft urged American women to get involved in politics just as she had—although she stopped short of encouraging them to seek office in

their own right—and she spoke out in favor of higher education for women and for the suffrage movement. To Americans expecting a more traditional first lady, however, Nellie Taft was judged as too aggressive. News that she sat in on cabinet meetings and influenced her husband's decisions resulted in her being known in Washington circles as the "co-president"; these activities did not sit well with the average American who believed a woman's place was in the home and the role of the president's wife was social, not political.

Mrs. Taft brought the first automobiles to the White House and insisted that the president and his family have a fleet of the finest new cars at their disposal. She designed a beautiful outdoor reception area in which she hosted regular parties featuring musical entertainment. The most memorable of her receptions was the one in honor of her silver wedding anniversary—perhaps a tribute to the anniversary party that had inspired her very first White House ambitions.

Mrs. Taft was, in the eyes of more traditional Americans, too ambitious and too opinionated for a woman. In another time, she would have likely sought public office in her own right; but at the turn of the century that option was not available, and she was left with the difficult position of living out her ambitions through her husband. After leaving the White House, the Tafts remained in Washington, where William Taft finally received the Supreme Court appointment he had long awaited. Nellie Taft died in 1943 and is buried in Arlington National Cemetery next to her husband.

William Howard Taft proved his devotion to his wife just two months into his term as president, when Nellie suffered a stroke and was for many months incapacitated by impaired speech. President Taft spent long hours by her side; with his help and that of her sisters, who took on her social responsibilities, Mrs. Taft soon regained her speech and was back on her feet. The Tafts, pictured together at left, were married forty-four years and raised two sons and a daughter.

Mrs. Taft's most visible and lasting contribution to Washington is celebrated each spring as the capital's beloved cherry trees display their beautiful blossoms. In March of 1912, Nellie Taft and the wife of the Japanese ambassador planted the first of what would be more than three thousand Japanese cherry trees along Washington's Tidal Basin.

ELLEN AXSON WILSON
1860–1914
WOODROW WILSON ADMINISTRATION 1913–1921

Ellen Axson Wilson, wife of President Woodrow Wilson, was a striking change from the previous first lady, Nellie Taft, who had been full of political ambition and enthralled by the potential power of her position. Mrs. Wilson, like many of her predecessors, saw the White House as a family home and her primary role as that of mother to her three daughters and wife to her husband. Mrs. Wilson was not unaware, however, of the unique opportunity her position afforded; she believed that the first lady had the responsibility to work on social issues. Unfortunately, after less than a year and a half in the White House, Ellen Wilson died of Bright's disease.

Born in May of 1860 in Savannah, Georgia, Ellen Axson was a sensitive and refined woman with a talent for painting and an interest in music and literature. She married Woodrow Wilson on June 24, 1885.

Mrs. Wilson spent much of her brief time in the White House painting and drawing in an attic studio. She had worked previously as a professional painter, but as first lady she donated her work to be auctioned for charity. As an outgrowth of her own interest in art, Mrs. Wilson devoted a room of the White House to the display of craftworks by the women of the Blue Ridge Mountains. One of Mrs. Wilson's more public projects was her work to improve the condition of the poor neighborhoods of Washington, D.C. The first lady took congressmen on tours of the city's bleakest areas and initiated legislation aimed at eliminating the slums. Mrs. Wilson did not, however, see her role as truly political—a woman of grace and refinement, she simply understood that while she desired to live essentially as a private citizen, she could not ignore the great opportunity to do good that was inherent in her public position. Ellen Wilson is buried in her Georgia hometown.

Ellen and Woodrow Wilson had three daughters—Margaret, Jessie, and Eleanor—two of whom were married in the White House. The children were Ellen's greatest love. She had given up a career as an artist when she became a mother, for she plainly stated that "three daughters take more time than three canvases." Ellen Wilson and her daughters are pictured at left at the White House.

Ellen Wilson was without pretensions. "A person would be a fool to have his head turned by externals," she once remarked about the trappings of her position as first lady. Her core belief was that she was a private individual. To Ellen Wilson, the position of first lady was a privilege that came with responsibilities, not power. Ellen Wilson is pictured above with President Wilson.

EDITH BOLLING GALT WILSON

1872–1961

WOODROW WILSON ADMINISTRATION 1913–1921

Edith Bolling Galt met President Woodrow Wilson shortly after the 1914 death of his first wife, Ellen. Mrs. Galt's friendship led the president out of his deep grief; and by December of the following year, they were married. The news of their union, since it came just over a year after the death of the beloved Ellen Wilson, met with much public disapproval. By the end of President Wilson's second term, however, Edith Galt Wilson's undying devotion to her husband and her courage and patriotism during a time of national crisis would quiet those who questioned the propriety of the marriage.

Edith Bolling was born in Wytheville, Virginia, in 1872. She was an intelligent and well-educated widow of forty-three when she met President Woodrow Wilson through a mutual friend. Edith weathered well the scandals surrounding their marriage, for she had come to believe that she and Woodrow Wilson were destined to be together and to lead the country. In the White House, Edith eschewed traditional social duties to concentrate on working side by side with her husband. In the tradition of James and Sarah Polk, the Wilsons developed a true working partnership. Edith Wilson never liked the term first lady—she always referred to herself as Mrs. Woodrow Wilson, a symbol of her great devotion to her husband. The two were rarely separated, and Mrs. Wilson was the president's assistant and his most trusted advisor.

When the United States entered World War I, Edith Wilson's devotion to the work of the presidency became a national asset. She was an example and an inspiration to the American people as she observed the rationing and other restrictions—enduring wheatless, meatless, gasless, and heatless days—necessitated by the war. In a memorable symbolic gesture, Mrs. Wilson replaced part of the White House grounds crew with a small flock of sheep that grazed on the lawn. With workers in short supply, the move saved manpower, and the wool from the sheep was auctioned off for charity.

Mrs. Wilson's greatest contribution to her country came after the war. When President Wilson suffered a debilitating stroke in September of 1919, she confidently and surreptitiously took charge to ensure that her husband's authority would not be usurped. Edith Wilson screened all of the president's visitors, calls, correspondence, and other business. She did not assume the role of the president, and she always insisted that she made no decisions on her own; she only made it possible for her husband to continue in his role.

In 1921, the Wilsons retired to their private home in Washington, D.C., where Woodrow Wilson died in 1924. Edith lived nearly forty more years, long enough to attend the inauguration of President John F. Kennedy. She died in 1961 and is buried beside her husband in Washington National Cathedral.

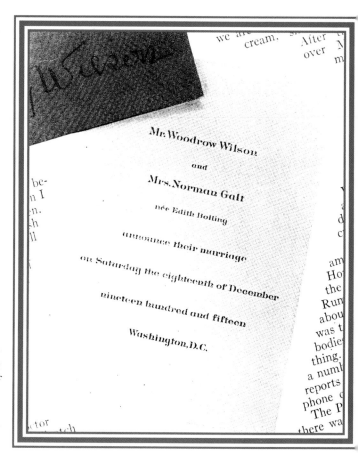

The wedding of President Woodrow Wilson and Edith Galt took place at the Washington home of the bride on December 18, 1915. The engagement met with much criticism, and Wilson offered Mrs. Galt the chance to back out of the marriage at the last minute to save her the public disapproval; but Mrs. Galt was devoted to the president and committed to their marriage. The ceremony was witnessed by forty relatives and friends and was followed by two weeks at Hot Springs, Arkansas. At right is the Wilsons' wedding invitation.

As a wealthy widow living alone in Washington after the turn of the century, Edith Galt became a successful, independent business woman. She revived her first husband's failing jewelry store, turned it into a profitable business, and later had the distinction of being the first woman in the capital to own and drive her own automobile.

FLORENCE KLING HARDING
1860–1924
WARREN G. HARDING ADMINISTRATION
1921–1923

Warren G. Harding once remarked of his wife that "Mrs. Harding wants to be the drum major in every band that passes." Like Sarah Polk and Nellie Taft before her, Florence Harding was an ambitious, driven woman who sought the role of first lady openly and vigorously. Unlike her two equally determined predecessors, however, Mrs. Harding did not have the benefit of a happy or stable marriage. Her years in the White House were on one hand the fulfillment of a dream and on the other a painful personal ordeal.

Florence, or Flossie, Kling De Wolfe was a thirty-year-old divorced mother of one when she met Warren Harding in her hometown of Marion, Ohio, in 1890. The two were married the following year. Mrs. Harding, who had studied for a time at the Cincinnati Conservatory of Music and taught piano after her divorce to support herself and her son, took over the management of her new husband's newspaper, the *Marion Star*. As circulation manager, Mrs. Harding found she had a talent for business as she helped turn the paper into a success and her husband into an influential public figure. As his political rise began, Mrs. Harding came to believe that she and her husband were destined for the White House, and she worked tirelessly toward that end.

When her husband received the presidential nomination in 1920, Flossie Harding became the most active female campaigner America had yet seen. In the very first presidential election where women's right to vote was backed by law, Mrs. Harding urged her husband to appeal directly to the female vote; and she urged the women themselves to get involved not just in voting, but in running their own country.

As first lady, Flossie remained as bold and forceful as ever. She gave public speeches and frequent press interviews and actively supported feminist causes. It was common knowledge that it was Flossie who had the driving ambition in the marriage, a fact that was often parodied in political cartoons and that won the couple the nickname of "The Chief Executive and Mr. Harding." Warren Harding's presidency was rocked by scandals—both political and personal—and there was a longstanding distance between him and his wife. With neither children to raise—her only son by her first marriage was by then living on his own— nor a stable marriage to fall back on, Flossie concentrated on work. She revived the weekly White House concerts by the Marine Band and the annual Easter egg roll. She also began hosting regular garden parties on the White House grounds. One of her most famous garden parties was one given for a group of wounded veterans. Mrs. Harding had begun a regular practice of visiting the wounded soldiers at a local hospital—she read to them, wrote letters for the disabled, distributed food and gifts, and was inundated with requests for help from veterans across the country.

Mrs. Harding never achieved broad popularity as first lady, despite her devotion to the role and her many innovations. She was criticized for her ambition and her lack of refinement—she was often overdressed, overly made-up, and overbearing—and her husband's failure as a president reflected poorly on her public image. Flossie Harding died in Marion, Ohio, in 1924, a little over a year after Warren Harding's death in office.

"Mrs. Harding in those days ran the show," remarked one of the first lady's former employees at her husband's newspaper in Ohio. The statement might be applied to everything Mrs. Harding pursued—she was ambitious and driven and confident. Flossie Harding was born on August 15, 1860, in Marion, Ohio. She was married for the first time at the age of nineteen and divorced six years later. She had only one child, a son born during her first marriage to Henry De Wolfe. The extent of Flossie Harding's involvement in her husband's presidential campaign was unprecedented for a woman. At the Republican convention in 1920, Flossie gave frequent interviews to the press and personally sought out undecided delegates to try and turn them toward her husband.

GRACE GOODHUE COOLIDGE
1879–1957
CALVIN COOLIDGE ADMINISTRATION 1923–1929

After the dark days of World War I and the political and personal scandals of the Harding administration, the American people embraced charming Grace Coolidge, wife of President Calvin Coolidge, as the ideal first lady. Nicknamed "Sunshine" by her own staff, the friendly, extroverted Mrs. Coolidge was the perfect balance to her taciturn husband, known as "Silent Cal." A devoted wife and mother, a gracious hostess, a college-educated woman who nonetheless saw her role as social and not political, Grace Coolidge was a perfect match to her times and a very successful first lady.

Born in Burlington, Vermont, in 1879, Grace Anna Goodhue was a recent graduate of the University of Vermont working as a teacher at the Clarke Institute for the Deaf in Northampton, Massachusetts, when she met a young attorney named Calvin Coolidge in 1903. Within two years, Grace and Calvin were married. Over the next two decades the Coolidges had two sons, and Calvin's political career progressed from a Northampton law practice to the Massachusetts governor's office in Boston and then to Washington and the vice presidency.

When Calvin Coolidge assumed the presidency upon the death of Warren Harding in 1923, Grace Coolidge was both excited and humbled by her new role. "Daily," she wrote, "I am impressed again with the responsibility and the opportunity which has been given me." Mrs. Coolidge strongly believed, as did her husband, that the responsibilities of the first lady did not include the work of governing. They believed that the president's wife was uniquely positioned to set an example for the people of America, and Mrs.

Coolidge felt strongly that part of that example must be work on social issues. Grace Coolidge's interest in education for the deaf continued in the White House, and she did much to promote the cause; she always insisted, however, that the cause and not her work be emphasized. Mrs. Coolidge also worked on issues of children's welfare, again quietly and mostly anonymously. She was not anonymous, however, when it came to entertaining or meeting the public. Grace Coolidge was the most visible first lady to date in American history. She daily took time to pose for pictures with visiting individuals and groups and made countless public appearances. Although she enjoyed formal entertaining, she was at her best meeting the common citizens of America, whether it was at a baseball game, the White House Easter Egg Roll, or in the department stores of New York, where she loved to shop. Intelligent and athletic, Mrs. Coolidge was a "modern woman" who nonetheless did not forsake the traditional roles of wife and mother. When the Coolidge's sixteen-year-old son, Calvin, Jr., died suddenly in 1924, citizens of all ages and political beliefs grieved along with their beloved first lady.

Grace and Calvin Coolidge left the White House just before the onset of the Great Depression and returned to Northampton. Calvin Coolidge died in 1933; his wife lived almost twenty-five years longer. She remained involved in the advancement of education of the deaf and, during World War II, took an active role in the Red Cross and other relief agencies. Grace Goodhue Coolidge died in 1957 and is buried beside the former president in Plymouth, Vermont.

Grace Coolidge, pictured at right with her collie, Rob Roy, loved children and animals and was a true humanitarian. Her extensive involvement in children's welfare issues remains an inspiration to first ladies to this day. Mrs. Coolidge lent her support to the Association for the Aid of Crippled Children, Children's Hospital, the Campfire Girls, the Girl Scouts, the Red Cross, and Christmas Seals. Her concern for children likely grew out of her love for her own children and her early career as a teacher of the deaf. After a visit to the White House, Helen Keller commented that the first lady was "responsive to every human need."

LOU HENRY HOOVER
1874–1944
HERBERT HOOVER ADMINISTRATION 1929–1933

First lady Lou Henry Hoover, like her husband, thirty-first president Herbert Hoover, was in many ways a victim of circumstance. She became the first lady in March of 1929; just over six months later, the stock market crashed, the Great Depression began, and in a matter of months, as the mood of the country turned angry and desperate, the Hoovers found themselves out of favor.

Lou Henry came to Washington with perhaps more education and more leadership experience than any woman before her. Born in Waterloo, Iowa, in 1874, she grew up in California where she spent her days hunting, camping, and horseback riding with her father. She attended Stanford University as the only female in the mining department. It was there that she met fellow mining major Herbert Hoover. After her graduation—Lou Henry was the first woman in America to earn a college degree in mining—Lou and Herbert were married and set off for China, where he had taken a job as a mining engineer. For the next three decades the Hoovers lived in China, England, Australia, New Zealand, Burma, and Russia. Lou Henry mastered the Chinese language and used her skills in Latin to work with Herbert on a translation of an ancient mining and metallurgy dictionary. During World War I, the Hoovers won international prominence for their work coordinating relief efforts for refugees in Belgium.

When the Hoovers returned to the United States, while her husband served as secretary of commerce, Lou became active in the women's rights movement. A firm believer in the benefits of physical exercise, Mrs. Hoover founded the National Women's Athletic Association to encourage young women to participate in sports. She also served as national president of the Girl Scouts and was active in the League of Women Voters, the American Association of University Women, and the National Geographic Society. Lou Hoover received honorary degrees from several prestigious universities and spoke often to groups of American girls and young women about careers and independence. In addition to all of her outside activities, Mrs. Hoover was a devoted mother to her two sons. She seemed, in fact, poised to become an inspirational first lady, an example of the great untapped

Lou Hoover, pictured above working in the garden in her Girl Scout leader's uniform, was devoted to the Girl Scouts, both before she became first lady and during her term in the White House. She first became a troop leader in 1917; five years later she was elected as the group's national president. She believed that involvement in the Girl Scouts encouraged young girls to get involved in community activity and physical activity. For a woman of her era, Lou Hoover held the unusual view that women should be given equal opportunity for involvement in competitive sports.

potential of the American woman.

From the start, however, Lou Hoover seemed uncertain of her role as first lady. Hesitant to assume too much leadership given her unofficial status, she instead cut short her activism. A fifty-five-year-old grandmother when she moved into the White House, Mrs. Hoover assumed a much more traditional role than her life experience would have predicted. She enjoyed entertaining and seemed confident and comfortable as a hostess, but backed off on many of the causes that had held her commitment before. As the Depression worsened, Mrs. Hoover seemed to retreat from the public eye even further. Privately she is said to have been sensitive and truly moved by the plight of the American people, but none of this translated to the public. As the months passed, Mrs. Hoover, like her husband, became a symbol of the nation's suffering. Lou Hoover and her husband left the White House in 1933 with public opinion rallied against them. She died in New York City in 1944 and is buried alongside Herbert Hoover in West Branch, Iowa.

Born on October 11, 1884, Anna Eleanor Roosevelt was a shy and serious child who showed little inclination toward leadership. A niece of President Theodore Roosevelt, Eleanor was raised by her maternal grandfather after her mother died when she was eight years old and her father proved unreliable due to his battle with alcoholism. Eleanor began to emerge from her shell after attending a private boarding school in London, but when she met her fifth cousin Franklin Roosevelt in 1902, nineteen-year-old Eleanor was still withdrawn and quiet. Franklin—an outgoing, charming Harvard undergraduate—seemed the antithesis of his cousin, but the two developed a close friendship. In 1905, despite the strong objections of his mother, they were married.

ANNA ELEANOR ROOSEVELT
1884–1962
FRANKLIN D. ROOSEVELT ADMINISTRATION 1933–1945

Eleanor Roosevelt understood something that Lou Hoover was never able to grasp—the problems of the Depression were not problems of economics alone, but of confidence and spirit. To desperate unemployed veterans—or to any of the countless Americans suffering through lack of work, lack of food, lack of housing, or lack of money—the symbolic gesture of solidarity was important. Eleanor Roosevelt proved from her very first day in the White House that she was a woman to match the times.

First Lady Eleanor Roosevelt had come a long way from the quiet, withdrawn woman who married Franklin Roosevelt in 1905. The Roosevelts had six children during the first ten years of their marriage, five of whom survived. Eleanor, of necessity, developed the self-confidence to stand her ground against her domineering mother-in-law and to raise her children while her husband's energies were devoted to his promising political career. By 1920, Franklin was a candidate for the vice-presidency; but the following year, he was stricken with polio. Eleanor's new-found confidence now faced a greater challenge. At home, she worked devotedly to nurse her husband back to health and fought his mother's demands that he give up

When jobless veterans marched on Washington in 1932, demanding early payment of their Veteran's bonuses, first lady Lou Hoover had sandwiches and coffee sent to them on her behalf but remained in the safety of the White House. Eleanor Roosevelt, the first lady who succeeded Mrs. Hoover, got in a car and rode over to speak to the veterans herself. Both women were motivated by compassion, but

public life. She also overcame her fear of public speaking in order to fill in for her husband and keep his name in the political ring. Thanks in part to his wife's devotion, in 1929, Franklin became governor of New York, and Eleanor herself became a recognized public figure. Four years later, Franklin Roosevelt was elected president of the United States.

Eleanor Roosevelt quickly became the most active, most visible, and most influential first lady America had ever known. Forty-eight years old and full of boundless energy, Mrs. Roosevelt threw herself into the job of rebuilding American confidence and promoting her husband's New Deal policies. She was known as Franklin's "eyes and ears" as she traveled tirelessly across the nation to meet the people and see firsthand the pain and suffering of the times. Eleanor Roosevelt averaged 40,000 miles per year as first lady, covering the nation by road, rail, and air. Her reports to Franklin on what she saw became his lifeline to the American people.

When World War II was added to the burden of the American people, Eleanor rose once more to the cause. She visited war zones across the globe and continued to exert a powerful influence on her husband, with whom she had a unique and devoted relationship. Franklin always respected Eleanor's opinions and was thankful for her involvement in and devotion to his work. Mrs. Roosevelt became the most popular and visible woman in America, chosen in poll after poll as one of the "most admired women in America." In twelve years in the White House, Eleanor Roosevelt redefined the role of the first lady. She was, in the minds of many Americans, more qualified to be president than the president himself. Eleanor Roosevelt became an American institution. "Sometimes I feel," she remarked, "like I am dressing the Washington Monument." She was right–to Americans, Eleanor Roosevelt was not merely the first lady, she was a national monument.

The Depression and World War II called on Americans to be brave and patriotic, and to work tirelessly and unselfishly for the national cause. Eleanor Roosevelt was an inspirational example. Introspective and humble, but also proud and confident, Mrs. Roosevelt gave energy to the nation. She was criticized by some who thought she had far overstepped her bounds as first lady, but she was embraced by most who were thankful for her leadership and inspiration. After Franklin's death in 1945, Eleanor moved to New York City but remained a part of American political life. In 1946, President Truman appointed her to the United Nations, where she served as chairman of the Commission on Human Rights. Eleanor Roosevelt died in 1962 and is buried next to her husband near the Roosevelt family home in Hyde Park, New York.

Eleanor and Franklin Roosevelt had one daughter, Anna, and four sons—James, Elliott, Franklin, Jr., and John. The president and first lady are pictured at right in a photo taken in the White House during one of their many Christmases there. Included are the children and their spouses, as well as grandchildren and other extended family members.

ELIZABETH WALLACE TRUMAN
1885–1982
HARRY S TRUMAN ADMINISTRATION 1945–1953

When Bess Truman was asked with which of the first ladies she most identified, her reply was Elizabeth Monroe. Her answer shows a good grasp of history and of her own impossible situation. Elizabeth Monroe followed Dolley Madison; Bess Truman followed Eleanor Roosevelt. Like Mrs. Monroe, Mrs. Truman had the self-confidence to define the role by her own standards despite the larger-than-life profile of her predecessor.

Like so many women who filled the role before her, Bess Truman did not want or expect to be the first lady. Her husband's ascension to the presidency was quick and unexpected; what Bess Truman wanted was for the family—she and Harry and daughter Margaret—to return to Independence, Missouri, for a quiet retirement. Born Elizabeth Virginia Wallace in Independence in 1885, Bess met Harry Truman in Sunday school while both were children. They did not begin their courtship for almost thirty years, however, and were not married until 1919. Bess was frugal and practical like her husband but had none of his political ambition. She preferred private family life in Independence; and when his election to the Senate moved the family to Washington, they rented an inexpensive apartment, furnished it practically and cheaply, and continued to live as they always had.

Bess Truman was sixty years old when she became first lady in 1945. The country mourned the death of Franklin Roosevelt, their leader for twelve years, and the departure of Eleanor Roosevelt, the woman who had inspired them and revolutionized her role. Eager to know more about Eleanor's replacement, reporters hounded Bess with questions. Her answers were a sign of things to come. "You don't need to know me," Mrs. Truman replied, "I'm only the president's wife and the mother of his daughter." When asked what character traits she thought essential to being first lady, she answered, "Good health and a well-developed sense of humor." Her subsequent remarks were few and far between. In fact, so little known was the new president's wife that at Christmas, nine months after her husband took office, Bess Truman shopped unrecognized in the department stores of Washington.

Mrs. Truman handled her affairs at the White House much as she had all her life. She took over management of household expenses and ran the White House frugally and efficiently. She was a gracious, if reserved, hostess. Her response to frequent requests by visitors for souvenirs was to purchase a box of common buttons to give away; Eleanor Roosevelt had given away sterling silver White House spoons. And when the White House was renovated and redecorated from cellar to attic, Mrs. Truman made suggestions only for the decoration of the rooms used daily by herself and her husband and daughter. She felt it was not her place to impose her opinions on the remainder of the house and its future occupants.

Bess Truman adopted no causes as first lady, and she caused little controversy. Those close to the Trumans called her a "shrewd politician," but she kept this side of herself away from public notice. She had the unfailing devotion of President Truman, who referred to her as "the Boss" in public and was known to look to her for advice throughout his career. In 1949, with White House renovations in full swing, the Trumans moved to Blair House, a smaller residence across from the White House. Mrs. Truman found life there more satisfying; she was a gracious hostess in the White House, but was glad when the move to smaller quarters curtailed most of the first family's social duties. Bess Truman was happy to leave Washington in 1953 and finally begin the retirement in Independence she had long sought. Mrs. Truman died in 1982 at the age of ninety-seven, making her the longest lived first lady in American history. Bess and Harry Truman are buried side by side at the Truman Library in Independence.

Harry, Bess, and Margaret Truman, pictured at right, had a close, dependent relationship and were given the nickname "The Three Musketeers" by White House staff, a tribute to their devotion to one another. As a child, Bess Truman overcame the tragedy of her father's suicide and matured into a reserved, intelligent woman with a strong desire for privacy. So powerful was her need for privacy that she burned all the letters she had written to Harry while he was in the war. Thankfully, Mrs. Truman preserved the letters Harry had written to her, providing historians with a treasure chest of information about the former president.

MAMIE DOUD EISENHOWER
1896–1979
DWIGHT D. EISENHOWER ADMINISTRATION 1953–1961

Asked whether she was happy to be taking on the title of first lady, Mamie Eisenhower answered without hesitation, "What American woman wouldn't want her husband to be the President?" As always, it was Ike who came first with Mamie. Without any of the self-doubt and uncertainty about her role that plagued so many of her predecessors, Mamie Eisenhower moved into the White House in 1953 and proudly called herself a housewife, admitting that the 1952 election had been the first in which she had voted. With her warm, unaffected manner, she won the affection of a nation devoted to peace and prosperity.

Marie Geneva Doud was born in Boone, Iowa, in November of 1896. Known from childhood as Mamie, she grew up comfortably in family homes in Iowa, Colorado, and Texas. It was in San Antonio that Mamie, just out of Miss Wolcott's finishing school, met young Dwight Eisenhower. Dwight and Mamie were married on July 1, 1916. In the thirty-seven years between their wedding and their move into the White House, the Eisenhowers never lived in a permanent home of their own. They moved twenty-eight times as Dwight rose through the ranks to become a five star general and an international hero during World War II while Mamie managed their household affairs and raised their son. Before 1952, neither of the Eisenhowers had any political interest or ambition; in November of that same year—on a wave of popularity that grew out of his wartime heroism—Dwight Eisenhower was elected to the presidency, and he and Mamie began what would be eight years as president and first lady.

Mamie Eisenhower was warm, spontaneous, and spirited. She loved Broadway musicals, expensive gowns, television, fried chicken, and, most of all, the color pink—pink paint on the walls, pink carpets on the floors, pink linens on the beds and in the bathrooms, and pink clothes filling her closets. She shocked the staff by conducting her daily morning meetings from her bed and interrupted her business every day to watch the soap opera "As the World Turns." Mamie loved to entertain and was a popular hostess. Her specialty was holiday parties, for which she had the White House decorated in the appropriate theme.

Still, for all her frivolity, Mamie Eisenhower was a woman of spirit and substance. During her husband's frequent illnesses she was constantly by his side; she lifted his spirits and bolstered the confidence of the people. She adopted no causes, but answered personally each piece of mail that came to her—some looking for help with a specific problem, others simply wanting to hear from the first lady—and acknowledged every one of the countless get-well cards her husband received while ill. Insiders say that Mamie worked a powerful influence on her husband and that when she had her mind set on something, she was stubborn and forceful. There is no doubt that her popularity with the American people bolstered Ike's own public image and helped him win two terms as president.

The fifties were a quiet time in American history; most of the world was at peace after the two decades of depression and war, and there was a calm before the coming storm of the sixties. Mamie Eisenhower was the perfect woman for the era. Dwight Eisenhower called her "my invaluable, my indispensible, . . . my lifelong partner." After they left the White House in 1961, the Eisenhowers moved to the first permanent, private home they had ever occupied on a full-time basis as a family, a farm in Gettysburg, Pennsylvania. Mrs. Eisenhower died in 1979 and is buried alongside her husband at the Eisenhower Library in Abilene, Kansas.

The first lady posed for this portrait while dressed in her trademark pink. Mrs. Eisenhower, no politician, was nonetheless a powerful force in her husband's campaign for the presidency. She traveled by train with Ike—who wore a campaign button that proclaimed "I like Mamie"—across the country and appeared at every stop to hand out buttons and greet her many admirers. The campaign train, known as the Eisenhower Special, visited forty-five states and made eighty different stops.

Jacqueline Kennedy so charmed the people of Paris on a visit there with the president that her husband uttered the now famous line identifying himself as "the man who accompanied Jackie Kennedy to Paris." Wherever she traveled with her husband, it was Jackie that the people wanted to see. Fluent in several languages, she spoke Spanish to the crowds of admirers in Mexico and translated the words of French leaders for her husband. Mrs. Kennedy eventually turned her life-long love of language into a career as an editor in New York City.

Mrs. Kennedy's devotion to the restoration of the White House left a valuable and lasting legacy. She established a Fine Arts Committee to oversee the project, put together a book on White House history to raise money for the renovations, and solicited donations of antiques from the public. An outgrowth of her project was the foundation of the White House Historical Association, devoted to the ongoing project of maintaining the president's home as an important piece of American history. Today, the preservation of White House history is an organized and professional effort. When the restoration was complete, Mrs. Kennedy hosted a televised tour of the new rooms that was watched by forty-six million Americans.

JACQUELINE BOUVIER KENNEDY ONASSIS

1929–1994
JOHN F. KENNEDY ADMINISTRATION 1961–1963

Thirty-one-year-old Jacqueline Bouvier Kennedy was the youngest first lady to occupy the White House, second only to Frances Cleveland. A devoted mother, a loyal supporter of her husband, and a woman of great intelligence and charm, Mrs. Kennedy—who believed it was the duty of the first lady to "contribute something" to American history—had only two- and-one-half years in the White House before assassination ended her husband's presidency and his life. In that short time, her grace and courage left a lasting impression upon the American people.

Born on July 18, 1929, in Southampton, New York, Jacqueline Lee Bouvier was raised in wealth and refinement in New York City, Newport, Rhode Island, and Washington, D.C. She received an excellent private education and upon graduation from college took a job as the inquiring camera girl for the *Washington Times Herald.* Her job introduced her to some of the most prominent people in Washington, among them a young senator from Massachusetts, John F. Kennedy. Jackie was John Kennedy's date for the 1953 inaugural ball of President Dwight Eisenhower; later that same year, they were married. Only seven years later, John Kennedy won election to the presidency, and the young couple moved into the White House.

America's obsession with Jackie Kennedy began on inauguration day, when her simple beige suit and matching pillbox hat were reported almost as widely as the message of her husband's address. The "Jackie look"—pillbox hats, bouffant hair, sleeveless sheath dresses—became the rage across the nation as women ,caught up in the energy and the spirit of the Kennedy administration, went to great lengths to emulate the president's wife. But there was much more to Mrs. Kennedy than image, and she wasted little time getting to work in the White House. On her very first day in residence, Mrs. Kennedy began plans for what would become the consuming project of her years as first lady: a historically correct renovation of the White House, part of an overall effort to make the home of the president of the United States a "museum of our country's heritage." Mrs. Kennedy's other great vision was of the White House as a center for the arts. Entertainment during the Kennedy years featured classical music, ballet, and Shakespearean drama. Jackie's style was sophisticated but not stilted.

Above all else, however, Mrs. Kennedy was devoted to her children—the first young children to live in the White House since the Theodore Roosevelt administration. Mrs. Kennedy once said, "If you bungle raising your children, I don't think whatever else you do well matters very much."

With her children and her White House projects, Jackie Kennedy had little time for political involvement; her role in that sphere was as a private advisor to her husband and a loyal and enthusiastic supporter of his programs. When President John Kennedy was assassinated in November of 1963, the American people came to understand the true grace and courage of their first lady. Mrs. Kennedy took charge of the funeral arrangements and orchestrated a stately, solemn tribute to her husband; all the while she maintained her quiet composure. When she left the White House, Mrs. Kennedy remained devoted to her children and led a very private life to shield them from the public eye. For the remainder of her life, Jackie Kennedy was a symbol of both triumph and tragedy to the American people. She died in 1994 and is buried next to President Kennedy in Arlington National Cemetery.

LADY BIRD JOHNSON
1912–
Lyndon B. Johnson Administration 1963–1969

Lady Bird Johnson became first lady at a moment of great national tragedy. The nation had just lost its president to an act of violence; a popular first lady was now a grieving widow. While President Lyndon Johnson would struggle with the difficult times and never truly emerge from the dark early days of his administration to become a popular or successful leader, his wife Lady Bird would eventually find a cause to call her own and leave her unique imprint on the role of first lady.

Born Claudia Taylor in Karnack, Texas, in 1912, Mrs. Johnson was known from childhood as Lady Bird. She was a recent graduate of the University of Texas with a degree in liberal arts and journalism when she met Lyndon Johnson in 1934. Johnson proposed the day after their very first meeting, and they were married in November of that year. In the twenty-nine years of their marriage before Lyndon Johnson became president, Lady Bird Johnson turned an investment in a Texas radio station into a communications empire and a substantial fortune for her family. She also raised two daughters, managed the family homes in Washington, Houston, and the LBJ ranch in Texas, and was an active and important campaigner for her husband.

Lady Bird Johnson believed that as first lady her true public role was to make the White House "an island of peace" for the president. She listed her top priorities as serving as hostess and working for the advancement of her husband's programs. At a time when the country was suffering grief over the death of President Kennedy and turmoil over the Vietnam War and civil rights, Lady Bird Johnson remained bright and optimistic. She established a committee for the preservation of the White House to continue the work begun by Jackie Kennedy on White House restoration. Her inspiration was Eleanor Roosevelt, and like Mrs. Roosevelt, Lady Bird was a full political partner to her husband and traveled the country in support of his Great Society programs. She had a sign on her desk in the White House that reflected her basic philosophy of life. It read simply, "Can Do."

Lady Bird Johnson pursued a degree in journalism because she believed that newspaper men and women "went more places and met more interesting people and had more exciting things happen to them."

Before the environment was a popular cause, Lady Bird Johnson adopted the beautification and preservation of America's landscape as her personal crusade. The Highway Beautification Act—which restricted the placement of billboards along public roadways—was the centerpiece of her determined effort to bring ecological causes to the forefront of American thought. She also planted trees and flowers, established parks, and traveled over two hundred thousand miles across the country promoting the cause of protecting America's natural beauty.

After President Johnson left office, Lady Bird retired with him to the LBJ Ranch in Texas, but the cause that she had discovered while first lady remained a central part of her life. She founded the National Wildflower Research Center in the early 1980s, for which she received the Congressional Gold Medal. A woman who faced the difficult task of following Jackie Kennedy as first lady had discovered the truth that had eluded some of her predecessors and guided others—the key to success in the role is to act upon those matters closest to your heart.

Nicknamed "Lady Bird" in infancy by a nurse who called her "pretty as a ladybird," Claudia Taylor Johnson was raised by her father and an aunt after the death of her mother in 1917. She met Lyndon Johnson shortly after her graduation from the University of Texas and married him that same year. Despite the difficulties of her husband's administration, Mrs. Johnson won the respect and admiration of the American people with her devotion to the cause of preserving our natural heritage.

PAT RYAN NIXON
1912–1993
RICHARD NIXON ADMINISTRATION 1969–1974

Pat Nixon, the wife of President Richard M. Nixon, was a reserved, practical woman who believed that the greatest responsibility of the first lady was to serve as a symbol of dignified strength to the American people. Born Thelma Catherine Ryan in Ely, Nevada, on March 16, 1912, she was called Pat from childhood because of her father's Irish heritage and the proximity of her birth to St. Patrick's Day. Mrs. Nixon grew up in southern California where, after the deaths of both her parents during her teenage years, she worked her way through college and took a position as a teacher at Whittier High School. She married Richard Nixon on June 21, 1940.

After many long, difficult years at her husband's side through the frequent ups and downs of his political career, Pat Nixon assumed a low profile in the White House with her two teenage daughters, whom she counted as her closest friends. Mrs. Nixon occasionally enjoyed some aspects of her role, however. She was one of the only first ladies to make a habit of greeting tourists visiting the White House, and she made efforts to continue the work of Jackie Kennedy to make the White House a museum of American heritage. Mrs. Nixon's renovations made the president's house more accessible to all Americans, including the disabled, the blind, and the deaf. Often criticized as stiff and cold in public, Mrs. Nixon was at her best in one-on-one encounters with the people, and she made a devoted effort to personally sign every piece of mail that went out of the White House in her name. She was not an activist first lady, but she did support the cause of volunteerism. She urged every American to get involved in his or her community, stated that "our success as a nation depends upon our willingness to give generously of ourselves," and hosted countless volunteer groups at the White House. Mrs. Nixon also won the affection of people in America and abroad during her extended travels alone and with her husband. Pat Nixon visited thirty-nine of the fifty states in her husband's first term and made historic trips to Africa, the Soviet Union, and China.

In the end, however, Mrs. Nixon's efforts were overshadowed by the bitter protests over American involvement in the Vietnam War and by the Watergate scandal that led to her husband's resignation. During this most difficult time for her family, Pat Nixon was a model of grace under pressure; she never wavered in her quiet support of her husband and never became part of the tide of anger, bitterness, and deception that swept through Washington. When President Nixon resigned, he and Pat retired to San Clemente, California. Mrs. Nixon died in 1993 and is buried beside her husband in Yorba Linda, California, at the Richard Nixon Library and Birthplace.

Pat Nixon was the first president's wife to travel to Africa, where she met with the leaders of Liberia, Ghana, and the Ivory Coast. Mrs. Nixon did much for the relations between the United States and these African nations with her warm, comfortable, open-minded diplomacy. Later in her husband's term, Mrs. Nixon traveled to China, where once again she won the respect and admiration of her host country. Always accepting of different cultures, Mrs. Nixon was praised as a goodwill ambassador. One newspaper remarked that the American people, "denounced by enemy countries as being war-minded imperialists, could use some goodwill" of the kind Mrs. Nixon represented. Mrs. Nixon's international success was furthered later in her husband's term by a historic visit to the Soviet Union.

FELIX DE COSSIO

72

ELIZABETH BLOOMER FORD
1918–
GERALD FORD ADMINISTRATION 1974–1977

Betty Ford had no intention of becoming the first lady. In 1974, after almost a quarter of a century in Washington as the wife of Congressman Gerald Ford, and after raising her four children, Mrs. Ford looked forward to an active, happy retirement in their hometown of Grand Rapids, Michigan. Instead, after a series of events elevated her husband first to the vice-presidency and then to the presidency, Mrs. Ford found herself a resident of 1600 Pennsylvania Avenue. She may not have sought the position of first lady, but Betty Ford was not intimidated by the role. Candid and engaging, Mrs. Ford became a symbol of the changing times and a role model for women of all ages.

Born on April 8, 1918, in Chicago as Elizabeth Anne Bloomer, Betty Ford grew up in Grand Rapids with dreams of becoming a dancer. She studied for a while with Martha Graham in New York and also worked as a model before returning to Grand Rapids to take a position in a local department store. Betty met Gerald Ford in 1947. They were married in the midst of his first congressional campaign on October 15, 1948, and after Ford won election a few weeks later, they moved to Washington.

In her youth, Mrs. Ford had visions of a career as a dancer or a model; in her twenties she supported herself with her work as fashion coordinator in the Grand Rapids department store; in Washington, she had been a full-time wife, mother, and homemaker. As first lady, Betty Ford was uniquely positioned to understand the many different roles played by American women; in response to the growing support for the Equal Rights Amendment (ERA) and the influx of women into jobs outside of the traditional roles of wife and mother, she became a leading voice on women's issues. Mrs. Ford publicly supported the ERA and spoke out in favor of appointing a woman to the Supreme Court. She gave public speeches and lobbied congressmen, but most of all she spoke to the women of America who were caught in a confusing debate about work outside the home. Mrs. Ford spoke of the value of both the traditional role of women and the importance of opening up all opportunities for work to the female population. Her remarks on women's issues reveal a true sense of balance: "Whether . . . a career in the home or outside, what is important is that [each woman] make that decision herself—without any pressures to restrict her choice. . . . So what's all this about liberated women being career women? Anyone who feels good about what she's doing in the home should have the same sense of liberation."

Mrs. Ford also spoke candidly about issues in her own life, most importantly her battle with breast cancer. The first lady's public battle with the disease increased awareness and spurred women to seek better care for themselves. After she left the White House, Mrs. Ford, inspired by her own personal struggles, founded the Betty Ford Clinic for substance abuse, which has helped countless men and women overcome drug and alcohol dependency to lead more productive lives.

A New York Times *editorial remarked that if Betty Ford had done nothing else as first lady, "the light her trouble had shed on a dark subject would be contribution enough." The trouble of which they spoke was the first lady's battle with breast cancer. At a time when the disease was often kept secret and women were not informed about prevention and detection, Mrs. Ford spoke openly and honestly about her struggle with both the physical and emotional sides of cancer. Her battle with the disease began a new era of public awareness, and her courage served as an inspiration to countless others who faced cancer. It was this willingness to share her struggles for the good of others that allowed Mrs. Ford to admit to her struggle with alcohol addiction and open the Betty Ford Clinic, which has helped Americans of all ages and income levels to overcome debilitating addictions.*

74

ROSALYNN SMITH CARTER

Rosalynn Carter once said, "A first lady is in a position to know the needs of the country and do something about them." Mrs. Carter, wife of President Jimmy Carter, was faithful to this belief in the White House. Taking on the "eyes and ears" role pioneered by Eleanor Roosevelt, Rosalynn Carter was a tireless worker on behalf of the policies of her husband, the interests of the American people, and the causes that earned her special devotion.

Eleanor Rosalynn Smith was born on August 18, 1927, in Plains, Georgia. From childhood, she went by her middle name. Rosalynn's father died while she was young, and she worked during much of her childhood to help support her family. She spent two years at Georgia Southwestern College; and on July 7, 1946, nineteen-year-old Rosalynn married fellow Plains native Jimmy Carter, the brother of one of her closest childhood friends. For the next seven years the Carters lived outside of Georgia while Jimmy served in the navy. Rosalynn concentrated on raising their growing family but also took art and literature classes and enjoyed the opportunity that navy life gave them to see the rest of the country. In 1953, after the death of Jimmy's father, the Carters returned to their hometown to run the Carter family peanut business and begin Jimmy's political rise. From the start, Rosalynn was a partner to Jimmy in business and politics, as well as in the raising of their four children. They had a close,

balanced relationship, and Jimmy Carter counted his wife among his most trusted advisors.

When Jimmy Carter won the presidency in 1976, Rosalynn was eager to serve an active, informed, and meaningful role in his administration. Both Carters believed in the value of hard work and were guided by a strong faith. In many ways, they recalled an earlier southern couple in the White House, James and Sarah Polk. Rosalynn Carter traveled to Latin America as the president's special envoy, attended Cabinet meetings, and set up her own office in the East Wing of the White House. Mrs. Carter paid special attention to issues of mental health. She served on the President's Commission on Mental Health and testified in Congress about the issue. She also advocated, through her words and actions, community involvement for all Americans. Rosalynn Carter was a woman of boundless energy who believed in the power of public service. Unlike so many of her predecessors, she felt no need to hide her ambition or her involvement in her active husband's administration, and she made no apologies for being a woman equally committed to public service and family life.

In retirement, Rosalynn Carter has joined her husband in active involvement in the Habitat for Humanity program, which builds affordable housing across America for low-income families. She has also continued writing and speaking about her life and social causes.

Rosalynn Carter believed strongly in the necessity of women pursuing careers outside the home; she was a woman of action, and to her, the only way to assure equality was to live a life outside traditional gender roles. She lobbied throughout Washington for the appointment of more women to key government positions and actively supported ERA. Her office maintained a list of women with high qualifications for a broad range of government appointments and made that list available to all with the power of hiring. She saw clearly how the first lady's position must grow to match the times. "The role of the first lady has changed as the role of women has changed," she remarked, "I don't think any man who would be president of the United States would have a wife with no ambition . . . ."

Nancy Davis Reagan
1923–
Ronald Reagan Administration 1981–1989

Nancy Davis was a successful movie actress with eleven motion pictures to her credit when she met the president of the Screen Actors Guild, Ronald Reagan, in 1949. Three years later, on March 4, 1952, Ms. Davis gave up her promising career to marry Reagan. In the years to follow, Nancy Reagan was her husband's staunchest supporter as he rose from actor to governor of California to president of the United States.

Nancy Davis Reagan was born Anne Frances Robbins on July 6, 1923, in New York City. In 1929, her mother, an actress, remarried. Her new husband, Loyal Davis, moved the family to Chicago, where Nancy, as she was known, found a more stable life and eventually took her stepfather's surname. Nancy attended Smith College in Massachusetts, where she was a theatre major.

As first lady, Mrs. Reagan was a loyal defender of her husband and one of his most forceful and outspoken advisors. She came under some public criticism for her lavish spending on redecorating the White House family quarters and her practice of accepting gifts of expensive gowns from leading designers, and she was judged harshly by some within the White House who saw her as too opinionated and too powerful for her role.

Mrs. Reagan's most positive legacy to the role of first lady is her involvement in the fight against drug and alcohol abuse in children. Her slogan of "Just Say No" has become a part of the American vernacular, and her actions have done much to draw attention to the growing problem of substance abuse and addiction in America.

In retirement, Mrs. Reagan has continued as one of her husband's most loyal supporters. The mother of two children, she has written a biography and remained active in many of the causes that she became involved with in the White House.

Nancy Reagan, below in the White House and at right wearing her trademark red, was known for her elegance and style; some thought her style was excessive and inappropriate, others found it inspirational and fitting for her position. After the informality of the Carter administration, the Reagans brought an almost royal feel to the White House, which recalled the days of Angelica Van Buren and Julia Tyler. In fact, Nancy Reagan was dubbed "Queen Nancy" by members of the press. Since leaving the White House, Mrs. Reagan and her husband have lived in California, where she remains his staunchest supporter.

BARBARA PIERCE BUSH
1925–
GEORGE BUSH ADMINISTRATION 1989–1993

First Lady Barbara Bush once described her public image as that of "everybody's grandmother." Perhaps this explains her great appeal to the American people, who widely embraced her during the administration of her husband, forty-first president George Bush. Despite the changing tide of political opinion that eventually turned her husband out of office, Mrs. Bush remained a favorite of Americans of all ages and political leanings.

Born on June 8, 1925, in Rye, New York, Barbara Pierce was the daughter of prominent publisher Marvin Pierce. She was a sixteen-year-old student at Ashley Hall prep school when she met young George Bush at a Christmas dance in Connecticut in 1941. They were engaged that following summer, but delayed their marriage while George fought in World War II, piloting a plane he called *Barbara*, and Barbara worked in a nuts and bolts factory to support the war effort before she began studying at Smith College. When George completed his tour with the navy, Barbara dropped out of school, and they were married.

In the years that followed, the Bushes would have six children—one of whom, Robin, would die tragically of leukemia—and live in twenty-nine homes in seventeen cities. George pursued his career, first in the oil business and then in politics, and Barbara became a devoted, active wife and mother.

In the White House, Barbara Bush continued to put family first and focused on her grown children and her many grandchildren. She was known for her forthright manner, her quick wit, and her thoughtful, staunch support of her husband. Her love of her own children translated into public service work for the benefit of all children. Mrs. Bush was a supporter of Head Start and other education programs and also devoted a great deal of energy to the support of literacy programs. The Bush White House was a comfortable, family home; children and dogs were common sights, and Mrs. Bush's warm, down-to-earth manner was the ruling attitude.

Since her White House days, Mrs. Bush has continued to support the causes of literacy and education; but for the most part she has settled down to enjoy private life as a wife, mother, and grandmother.

The White House has undergone a continual process of change and renovation since the days of its first inhabitants, John and Abigail Adams. Much of the responsibility for that process has fallen to our first ladies. They have decorated in the style that suits their families' tastes and lifestyles and have held onto a long-standing tradition of keeping the White House a historically accurate museum of our American heritage as well as a family home. Barbara Bush brought to the White House an official style that matched her own personal style—elegant, yet understated and relaxed.

Barbara Bush's interest in literacy as first lady grew out of her own efforts to help her son Neil in his battle with dyslexia. When Mrs. Bush became first lady, over thirty-five million American adults were illiterate. She called the problem "the most important" one the country had and believed that many of our social ills would be lessened if more of our citizens had the reading and writing skills to make improvements in their own lives. The Barbara Bush Foundation for Family Literacy was founded in support of efforts to help families escape the prison of illiteracy.

HILLARY RODHAM CLINTON
1947–
BILL CLINTON ADMINISTRATION 1993–2001

First Lady Hillary Rodham Clinton brought revolutionary changes to the role in 1993–changes that reflect the status of women in her own and future generations. The first attorney to become first lady, she is a graduate of Wellesley College and Yale Law School. Her resume includes positions as an attorney for the Children's Defense Fund, a professor of law at the University of Arkansas, and a former member of a large corporate law firm in Arkansas. She is also a wife and mother who has, throughout her life, worked to balance the demands of her family and her career.

Hillary Rodham was born in Chicago on October 26, 1947. She met her future husband while both were students at Yale Law School. After their marriage, the Clintons moved to Arkansas, where Bill Clinton rose to the governor's office and Hillary pursued her career as an attorney. The Clintons have one daughter.

As first lady, Mrs. Rodham Clinton stirred controversy with the active role she assumed in her husband's administration, specifically as the head of his Task Force on National Health Care Reform. She was a visible, outspoken first lady and an inspiration to many women; others found her activism and her involvement in official government business inappropriate for an unelected public figure.

Mrs. Rodham Clinton established an office for herself in the West Wing of the White House, a move that demonstrated her belief that she and her husband were partners in the work of the presidency. In her eight years as First Lady, she tried to live up to her public statement that "we all have an obligation to give something of ourselves to our community." She focused her commitment to children, supporting measures to increase immunization of preschoolers, to

Hillary Rodham Clinton is the first president's wife born after World War II. She represents a new generation of women who were raised with a greater expectation of equality and who face the difficult task of pioneering a new definition for the role of first lady. A public figure in her own right throughout her career, Mrs. Rodham Clinton has worked on controversial issues as a lawyer for the Children's Defense Fund and as a staff lawyer for the House Judiciary Committee during the impeachment hearings of Richard Nixon. She has enlivened once more the debate about the proper role of the first lady as a non-elected individual. Mrs. Clinton likely enjoys the challenge; in her commencement address as a student at Wellesley College, Rodham Clinton stated that she viewed politics as the "art of making possible what appears impossible."

Although the role of the first lady has evolved through the years to include more official public and political duties, the traditional roles of hostess and homemaker have remained essential to the public image of the women of the White House. A first lady today is allowed, even required, to possess ambition and intelligence, but she is also expected to give equal attention to the more traditional matters of style and entertaining. Today's first ladies, however, unlike their earliest predecessors, come to the role willingly, as partners to their husbands and with the experiences of more than forty women to guide them. Despite all the changes, however, Hillary Clinton, who decorated the White House room pictured above, has found the greatest challenge to be the same that has existed since the days of Martha Washington—how to make the White House into a family home for herself, her husband, and their daughter while finding professional and personal satisfaction in the public aspects of her role.

expand health insurance coverage for all children, and to improve prenatal care. In 1996, Hillary Clinton published a book called *It Takes a Village and Other Lessons Children Teach Us,* which called for American society to take responsibility for the well-being of all its children. Mrs. Clinton also played a key role in the 1997 White House Conference on Early Childhood Development and Learning. She traveled extensively as first lady, serving as a goodwill ambassador in Europe, Asia, Africa, and Latin America.

In her final year as first lady, Hillary Clinton became a pioneer once again. In the winter of 2000,

Mrs. Clinton announced that she was to be a candidate for Senate from the state of New York. In preparation for the campaign, she and her husband purchased a home near New York City and the first lady took up permanent residence there, nearly a full year before the end of her husband's term as president. In November of 2000, Hillary Rodham Clinton won election to the Senate from the state of New York. Mrs. Clinton left behind the position of first lady and began a political career of her own, having enlarged and expanded the traditional role of the president's spouse.

LAURA WELCH BUSH
1947–
GEORGE W. BUSH ADMINISTRATION 2001–

Laura Welch Bush begins her residence in the White House no stranger to the title of first lady. For six years, while her husband George W. Bush was governor of Texas, Mrs. Bush served as that state's first lady, a role that prepared her well for the demands and responsibilities of being the wife of the president.

Like her husband, Laura Welch Bush was raised in Midland, Texas. From a young age, she set her sights upon a career in education. She earned a bachelor's degree in education from Southern Methodist University and later a master's degree in library science from the University of Texas. Upon completion of her education, Mrs. Bush taught elementary grades in the Dallas and Houston public schools for nearly a decade before her marriage to George Bush in 1977.

The mother of twin daughters, Mrs. Bush promises to bring a blend of the modern and the traditional to her years as first lady. Though a possessor of advanced degrees and an extensive professional career, Mrs. Bush, as first lady of Texas, did not seek an active role in her husband's administration. Laura Bush followed the model provided by her mother-in-law, former first lady of the United States Barbara Bush, and concentrated her efforts, and the spotlight of her position, on social issues, particularly education and literacy.

One of Mrs. Bush's central projects as first lady of Texas was to bring all Texas public school students to grade level or above in their reading skills with a program called the First Lady's Family Literacy Initiative. The initiative was funded in part by Barbara Bush's Foundation for Family Literacy. Laura Bush also worked to promote awareness of women's and children's health issues and began an annual Texas book festival to celebrate local authors and illustrators.

Mrs. Bush also concentrated her energies as first lady of Texas on issues of women's health and child health and safety. She was a member of the Governor's Spouse Program of the National Govenors Association, which worked to promote breast cancer awareness. She serves on the advisory board of the American Library Association's Office of Intellectual Freedom and is a member of the national advisory board of Reading Is Fundamental.

As first lady of the United States, Laura Bush has pledged to continue to promote education and literacy on a national level.

Laura and George W. Bush married in Laura's native town of Midland, Texas, in 1977. Four years later, their family expanded with the addition of twin daughters, Jenna and Barbara, who are named after their grandmothers. Mrs. Bush attributes her love for books, as well as her background as a teacher and librarian, as motivating forces for her literacy advocacy. From 1996 to 2000, during her time as the first lady of Texas, Mrs. Bush helped 325 Texas public libraries receive grants totaling $890,000.

PRESIDENTIAL ADMINISTRATIONS

George Washington administration 1789–1797
First Lady: Martha Dandridge Custis Washington
Born June 2, 1731, New Kent County, Virginia
Died May 22, 1802, Mount Vernon, Virginia

John Adams administration 1797–1801
First Lady: Abigail Smith Adams
Born November 1744, Weymouth, Massachusetts
Died 1818, Quincy, Massachusetts

Thomas Jefferson administration 1801–1809
First Lady: None
Wife: Martha Wayles Skelton Jefferson
Born 1748, Williamsburg, Virginia
Died September 6, 1782, Charlottesville, Virginia

James Madison administration 1809–1817
First Lady: Dolley Payne Madison
Born 1768, Piedmont, North Carolina
Died 1849, Washington, D.C.

James Monroe administration 1817–1825
First Lady: Elizabeth Kortright Monroe
Born 1768, New York, New York
Died September 23, 1830, Oak Hill, Virginia

John Quincy Adams administration 1825–1829
First Lady: Louisa Johnson Adams
Born 1775, London, England
Died 1852, Washington, D.C.

Andrew Jackson administration 1829–1837
First Lady: None
Wife: Rachel Donelson Jackson
Born 1767, Halifax County, Virginia
Died December 1828, Nashville, Tennessee

Martin Van Buren administration 1837–1841
First Lady: Angelica Van Buren (daughter-in-law)
Wife: Hannah Hoes Van Buren
Born 1783, Kinderhook, New York
Died February 5, 1819, Albany, New York

William Henry Harrison administration 1841
First Lady: Anna Tuthill Symmes Harrison
Born 1775, Long Island, New York
Died February 1864, North Bend, Ohio

John Tyler administration 1841–1845
First Lady: Letitia Christian Tyler
Born 1790, Cedar Grove Plantation, Virginia
Died September 10, 1842, Washington, D.C.
First Lady: Julia Gardiner Tyler (married June 26, 1844)
Born 1820
Died 1889, Richmond, Virginia

James K. Polk administration 1845–1849
First Lady: Sarah Childress Polk
Born 1803, Murfreesboro, Tennessee
Died 1891, Nashville, Tennessee

Zachary Taylor administration 1849–1850
First Lady: Margaret Mackall Smith Taylor
Born 1788, Calvert County, Maryland
Died August 18, 1852

Millard Fillmore administration 1850–1853
First Lady: Abigail Powers Fillmore
Born 1798, Saratoga County, New York
Died March 30, 1853, Washington, D. C.

Franklin Pierce administration 1853–1857
First Lady: Jane Means Appleton Pierce
Born 1806, Hampton, New Hampshire
Died 1863, Concord, New Hampshire

James Buchanan administration 1857–1861
First Lady: Harriet Lane (niece)
Born 1830, Franklin County, Pennsylvania
Died 1903, Washington, D.C.

Abraham Lincoln administration 1861–1865
First Lady: Mary Todd Lincoln
Born December 14, 1818, Kentucky
Died July 16, 1882, Springfield, Illinois

Andrew Johnson administration 1865–1869
First Lady: Eliza McCardle Johnson
Born 1810, Leesburg, Tennessee
Died 1876, Greeneville, Tennessee

Ulysses S. Grant administration 1869–1877
First Lady: Julia Boggs Dent Grant
Born 1826, St. Louis, Missouri
Died 1902, New York, New York

Rutherford B. Hayes administration 1877–1881
First Lady: Lucy Webb Hayes
Born August 1831, Chillicothe, Ohio
Died 1889, Fremont, Ohio

James A. Garfield administration 1881
First Lady: Lucretia Rudolph Garfield
Born 1832, Hiram, Ohio
Died 1918, Ohio

Chester A. Arthur administration 1881–1885
First Lady: Ellen Lewis Herndon Arthur
Born August 30, 1837, Culpepper Court House, Virginia
Died January 12, 1880, New York, New York

Grover Cleveland administration 1885–1889
First Lady: Frances Folsom Cleveland
Born 1864, Buffalo, New York
Died October 29, 1947, Baltimore, Maryland

Benjamin Harrison administration 1889–1893
First Lady: Caroline Scott Harrison
Born 1832, Oxford, Ohio
Died October 1892, Washington, D.C.

Grover Cleveland administration 1893–1897
First Lady: Frances Folsom Cleveland
Born 1864, Buffalo, New York
Died October 29, 1947, Baltimore, Maryland

William McKinley administration 1897–1901
First Lady: Ida Saxton McKinley
Born January 1847, Canton, Ohio
Died 1907, Canton, Ohio

Theodore Roosevelt administration 1901–1909
First Lady: Edith Kermit Carow Roosevelt
Born August 1861, Norwich, Connecticut
Died September 30, 1948, Oyster Bay, Long Island

William H. Taft administration 1909–1913
First Lady: Helen "Nellie" Herron Taft
Born 1861, Cincinnati, Ohio
Died May 22, 1943, Washington, D.C.

Woodrow Wilson administration 1913–1921
First Lady: Ellen Louise Axson Wilson
Born May 1860, Savannah, Georgia
Died August 6, 1914, Washington, D.C.
First Lady: Edith Bolling Galt Wilson
Born 1872, Wyethville, Virginia
Died December 28, 1961, Washington, D.C.

Warren G. Harding administration 1921–1923
First Lady: Florence Kling Harding
Born 1860, Marion, Ohio
Died November 21, 1924, Marion, Ohio

Calvin Coolidge administration 1923–1929
First Lady: Grace Goodue Coolidge
Born 1879, Burlington, Vermont
Died 1957, Northampton, Massachusetts

Herbert Hoover administration 1929–1933
First Lady: Lou Henry Hoover
Born 1874, Waterloo, Iowa
Died 1944, New York, New York

Franklin Delano Roosevelt administration 1933–1945
First Lady: Eleanor Roosevelt
Born October 11, 1884, New York, New York
Died November 1962, New York, New York

Harry S Truman administration 1945–1953
First Lady: Elizabeth "Bess" Virginia Wallace Truman
Born February 13, 1885, Independence, Missouri
Died 1982, Independence, Missouri

Dwight D. Eisenhower administration 1953–1961
First Lady: Marie "Mamie" Geneva Doud Eisenhower
Born November 1896, Boone, Iowa
Died November 1, 1979, Gettysburg, Pennsylvania

John F. Kennedy administration 1961–1963
First Lady: Jacqueline Lee Bouvier Kennedy
Born July 18, 1929, Southampton, New York
Died 1994, New York, New York

Lyndon B. Johnson administration 1963–1969
First Lady: Claudia "Lady Bird" Alta Taylor Johnson
Born 1912, Karnack, Texas

Richard M. Nixon administration 1969–1974
First Lady: Thelma Catherine "Pat" Ryan Nixon
Born March 16, 1912, Ely, Nevada
Died June 22, 1993, Park Ridge, New Jersey

Gerald R. Ford administration 1974–1977
First Lady: Elizabeth Ann "Betty" Bloomer Ford
Born April 8, 1918, Chicago, Illinois

Jimmy Carter administration 1977–1981
First Lady: Eleanor Rosalynn Smith Carter
Born August 18, 1927, Plains, Georgia

Ronald Reagan administration 1981–1989
First Lady: Nancy Davis Reagan
Born July 6, 1923, New York, New York

George Bush administration 1989–1993
First Lady: Barbara Pierce Bush
Born June 8, 1925, Rye, New York

William J. Clinton administration 1993–2001
First Lady: Hillary Rodham Clinton
Born October 26, 1947, Chicago, Illinois

George W. Bush administration 2001–
First Lady: Laura Welch Bush
Born 1947, Midland, Texas

Index

Photo Credits

From The White House Collection: **Page 4**: *Martha Dandridge Custis Washington*, by Eliphalet F. Andrews; acquired in 1878. **11**: *Dolley Payne Todd Madison*, by Gilbert Stuart; acquired in 1994. **15**: *Louisa Catherine Johnson Adams*, by Gilbert Stuart; acquired in 1971. **21**: *Julia Gardiner Tyler*, by Francesco Anelli; acquired in 1869. **37**: *Lucy Ware Webb Hayes*, by Daniel Huntington; acquired in 1881. **47**: *Edith Kermit Carow Roosevelt*, by Theobald Chartran; acquired in 1902. **49**: *Helen Herron Taft*, by Bror Kronstrand; acquired in 1943. **53**: *Edith Bolling Galt Wilson*, by Adolpho Muller-Ury; acquired in 1963. **57**: *Grace Anna Goodhue Coolidge*, by Howard Chandler Christy; acquired in 1924. **59**: *Lou Henry Hoover*, by Richard M. Brown after Philip de László; acquired in 1951. **60**: *Anna Eleanor Roosevelt Roosevelt*, by Douglas Chandor; acquired in 1965. **64**: *Mamie Geneva Doud Eisenhower*, by Thomas E. Stephens; acquired in 1961. **66**: *Jacqueline Bouvier Kennedy Onassis*, by Aaron Shikler; acquired in 1971. **69**: *Claudia Taylor (Lady Bird) Johnson*, by Elizabeth Shoumatoff; acquired in 1968. **71**: *Pat Ryan Nixon*, by Henriette Wyeth; acquired in 1981. **72**: *Elizabeth Bloomer Ford*, by Felix de Cossio; acquired in 1978. **74**: *Rosalynn Smith Carter*, by George Augusta; acquired in 1985. **77**: *Nancy Davis Reagan*, by Aaron Shikler; acquired in 1989. **78**: *The White House*. **79**: *Barbara Pierce Bush*, photograph by David Valdez. **80**: *Hillary Rodham Clinton*, photograph by Barbara Kinney. **81**: *Clinton White House Interior*.

From the Library of Congress: **Page 5**: *First Meeting; Washington's Courtship*. **7**: *Abigail Smith Adams*; LCUSZ62-24492. **8**: *Martha Wayles Skelton Jefferson*; LCUSZ60-24932. **9**: *Martha Jefferson Randolph;* LCUSZ62-13489. **10**: *Dolley Payne Todd Madison*; LCUSZ62-10447. **12**: *Elizabeth Kortright Monroe*; LCUSZ62-24493. **14**: *Louisa Johnson Adams*; LCUSZ62-14438. **16**: *Rachel Donelson Jackson*; LCUSZ62-100102. **15**: *Hannah Hoes Van Buren*; LCUSZ62-25776. **20**: *Letitia Christian Tyler*; LCUSZ62-13495. **22**: *Sarah Childress Polk*; LCUSZ62-7560. **24**: *Elizabeth Taylor Bliss*; LCUSZ62-25783. **25**: *Abigail Powers Fillmore*; LCUSZ62-1776. **26**: *Pierce Homestead*; LCUSZ62-36949. **29**: *Harriet Lane*; LCUSZ62-7893. **31**: (top) *Mary Todd Lincoln*; LCU62-707A. **31**: (bottom) *Lincoln at Home*; LCUSZ62-2072. **33**: *Eliza McCardle Johnson*; LC-Z62-25816. **34**: (top) *Julia Boggs Dent Grant*; LCUSZ62-4176. **34**: (bottom) *Ruins of Julia Grant Birthplace*. **39**: *Lucretia Rudolph Garfield*; LCUSZ62-25793. **40**: *Nell Arthur*; LCUSZ62-98155. **41**: *Ellen Herndon Arthur*; LCUSZ62-17135. **43**: *Frances Folsom Cleveland*; LCUSZ62-17635. **44**: *Caroline Scott Harrison*; LCUSZ62-97328. **45**: *Ida and William McKinley*; LCUS262-501834. **46**: *Roosevelt Family*; LCUSZ62-32238. **48**: *William and Helen Taft*; LCUSZ62-91029. **50**: *Ellen Wilson and Her Daughters*; LCUSZ62-17753. **51**: *Ellen and Woodrow Wilson*; LCUSZ62-17751. **52**: *Wedding Invitation*; LCUSZ62-33043. **54**: *Florence Kling Harding*; LCUSZ62-97729. **55**: *Florence Kling Harding*. **58**: *Lou Henry Hoover*, LCUSZ62-21334. **61**: *The Roosevelts at Christmas*; LCUSZ62-87957. **63**: *The Trumans*; LCUSZ62-71726. **67**: *Jacqueline Bouvier Kennedy Onassis*; LCUSZ62-21796. **68**: *Lady Bird Johnson*; LCUSZ62-723. **76**: *Nancy Davis Reagan*; LCUSZ62-94021.

From other sources: **Page 19**: *Anna Tuthill Symmes Harrison*, by Cornelia Stuart Cassady. Courtesy of the President Benjamin Harrison Home, Indianapolis, Indiana. **27**: *Jane Means Appleton Pierce*, daguerreotype owned by the Pierce Brigade, Concord, New Hampshire. **82**: Folio, Inc./Jeffrey MacMillan.

Editor's Note: The term "first lady," strictly speaking, refers to the wife of the president. Through the years, loyal daughters, nieces, and daughters-in-law have filled the role of White House hostess for bachelor or widower presidents and for those first ladies unable to fulfill their public duties. *First Ladies of the White House* considers the lives and contributions of these women and also of those wives who did not live to see their husbands elected to the presidency, in addition to the stories of the actual first ladies.